TOM SCHEERER

DECORATES

TOM SCHEERER
DECORATES

MIMI READ

PHOTOGRAPHS BY
FRANCESCO LAGNESE

THE VENDOME PRESS
NEW YORK

Contents

INTRODUCTION 7

City
PROPRIETY WITH APLOMB 19
NEW WAVE IN BROOKLYN HEIGHTS 31
ART AND DECORATING 41
CITY KIDS 51
PATRICIAN POLISH 59

Country
FARMHOUSE REDUX 69
AMERICAN SPLENDOR 85
SUMMER IN MAINE 99
A CLEAN CANVAS 117

Tropics
CONJURING OLD FLORIDA 131
PALM BEACH PIED-À-TERRE 153
GLAMOUR AND EXOTICA 163
THE SIMPLE LIFE 177
NATURAL SELECTIONS 187
ISLAND CHIC 207
LYFORD CAY CLUB 225

SOURCES 236
ACKNOWLEDGMENTS 239

Introduction

MEET TOM SCHEERER. He's 6'2", with textbook Anglo-Saxon good looks: snapping blue eyes, fair skin, a high forehead, and thick gray hair that sticks up and flops over. He's deftly, sometimes devastatingly verbal. His cerebral authority explains the nickname that an astute friend gave him years ago: Thomas Aquinas.

He loves old houses, contemporary art, Japanese baskets, maps, pot-au-feu, table manners, pink dahlias, dinner parties, coconut trees, beach stones, outdoor showers, and soap on a rope. He's self-deprecating, with aristocratic manners and a surprising grasp of street slang. He frequents the housewares department of the Dior store in Paris and regularly drops by Cove Landing, a cabinet of wonders in upper Manhattan where he shops for antiques. In Miami recently, he pulled his rental car to a halt on teeming Biscayne Boulevard to buy an intricate banana-leaf basket from the indigent hippie who made it. He still considers a trip to Ikea one of the sacraments.

Scheerer doesn't dress like other people. Decades ago, he devised a uniform for himself so that he would not have to think about clothing, and it is both wildly distinctive and utterly low-key: in winter it consists of vaguely Tyrolean wool jackets, wide-wale corduroy pants, and brown leather clogs with backs. In summer it's white pants and flip flops, even in Paris, where he tries to spend part of every month. His longtime partner, Michael, lives there full time in their renovated medieval building in the Marais, and Scheerer visits between jobs. They eat together glamorously at home. (Scheerer cooks and lights candles in their rustically cozy living room, its lopsided walls cross-sectioned with rubble and petrified wooden

OPPOSITE Coats of fresh paint have been applied and small changes have been made, but the Scheerer family's blue-and-white dining room in East Hampton still looks much the way it did after his grandmother first decorated it in 1946. Scheerer made the table to replace hers (his has a slightly larger top) and traded dilapidated cane-backed French chairs for loopy but sturdy wooden ones popularized by Frances Elkins. The painting over the fireplace is by Simon Parkes, Scheerer's brother-in-law. **ABOVE** Tom Scheerer on the lacquered-coral stairs in the East Hampton house. The hall was freshened with cheerful geranium wallpaper in the 1960s, when decorating was not yet a gleam in Scheerer's eye.

LEFT In Scheerer's fifteenth-century Paris house, the entrance features an elegant, long-legged Louis XVI oak console and a massive teak armoire he designed as a coat closet. The medieval staircase is configured around a four-story tree trunk with a spiraling handrail carved into it. RIGHT In the living room, Scheerer serves casual dinners at a black-painted Saarinen table pulled up to a Louis XV *canapé* with an assortment of chairs. On the mantelpiece, the wheel rim of an antique carriage is mounted as sculpture.

beams). Or else they go out to the most old-fashioned Paris restaurants imaginable, which please Scheerer no end.

Part artist, part crusty curmudgeon, and part solicitous alpha dog and family man, Scheerer has fast, blazingly confident opinions about anything to do with a house (and also the rest of life). If he likes some object or implement, exorbitant or humble, he's faithful to it for decades. He's capable of falling in love with a person, but also a coffee pot. If you opened the bedroom closet of his small apartment near Gramercy Park in Manhattan, you'd see forty or fifty lavender-and-white-checked cotton shirts stacked neatly on shelves, all seemingly the same. You would not see anything black.

Scheerer's decorating looks a great deal like him. It's tall and commanding but often quiet. It's smart, correct, breezy, chic, well edited—and just a touch eccentric. It balances refinement with all-American ease. Yet it is un-American in its emphasis on recycling, reinventing, and not overdoing things. The expression "decorated to death" never applies. Make no mistake: Scheerer's clients are plenty affluent (as all decorating clients are). But when you look at a Scheerer room, money is never your first (or your second or third) thought. In an age in which houses exhibiting unchecked exuberance, high drama, or conspicuous luxury get all the attention, he has cultivated his own more restrained brand of chic, a look he describes as "cheerful" and "no nonsense." But it is so much more.

"His early exposure to great houses and his architectural training really show," observes Stephen Drucker, former editor of *House Beautiful* and *Town & Country*, where he often published Scheerer's work. "He's like an Albert Hadley or a Van Day Truex, a human tuning fork with perfect pitch for space. He knows how to take the nervousness and restlessness out of a room. And he knows where money spent will make a real difference. When Tom says, 'Just do it,' you just do it."

Part of the alchemy is in the dynamic way Scheerer combines classicism, old-fashioned decorating, and a clean, modernist sensibility, much as David Hicks and Billy Baldwin did in their days. Hicks and Baldwin are two of Scheerer's favorite forebears in the trade, and he's always maintained that their frank, generous books (including *Billy Baldwin Decorates*) taught him most of what he knows about decorating. Hicks gave him the revolutionary notion that boldness can coexist with appropriateness. Baldwin made it clear that an unpretentious ease looks good on even the fanciest clients.

But Scheerer updates these masters by drawing on his own era and life experiences. He favors emphatically natural materials like pecky cypress, cork, and straw matting; vernacular crafts such as swirl-pattern Cuban cement tiles; found objects, including tinted or clear demijohns made into shimmering lamps; and the prettiest color combinations this side of India.

"The thing I love best about Tom's work is its wonderful polarities," says celebrated decorator Miles Redd. "It's spirited and reserved. It's exuberant and quiet. It's never, ever vulgar, thanks to his Yankee understatement, but you always notice it."

WHEN HE WAS IN HIS LATE THIRTIES, Scheerer bought his first house impulsively, on a one-day visit to Charleston to help one of his sisters house-hunt. The horrific July heat wave in progress might have caused other New Yorkers to think twice, but when Scheerer glimpsed the "for sale" sign on a clean-lined Colonial-era brick house with a walled garden, he was hooked.

Photographs of his Charleston house ran in *House & Garden* in 1997, and its dining room contained a trope that's still one of his signatures: a white laminate Eero

Scheerer's sparkling Charleston dining room appeared in *House & Garden*'s January 1997 issue. He played to the Charleston audience by using a traditional American camelback sofa and Chippendale-style chairs for seating but turned the room on its ear with high and low Saarinen tables in dialogue with each other.

Scheerer returned to Manhattan from Charleston by degrees, beginning in 1999. The pied-à-terre he designed for himself in Gramercy Park around that time has the scholarly feeling of an architect's lair. Two Crate & Barrel armchairs flank a Mies van der Rohe ottoman. The classic Hans Wegner wishbone chair is one of six in the apartment. A Japanese forged-iron salver rests on the black granite fireplace surround.

Saarinen table, the round top blooming from its slender stalk like the metaphysical idea of a table. It was pulled up to a vintage camelback sofa in white muslin. Six antique Chinese Chippendale chairs in mellowed red lacquer were scattered around it. This dining *mise en scene* crackled with a scrupulous critical intelligence, yet it felt sexy, breezy, and youthful. There was not a twinge of formality anywhere (in Scheerer's book, the kiss of death). Certainly it looked like nothing else being published at the time.

Scheerer's commingling of old-fashioned and modern sensibilities makes perfect sense. Born in New York and brought up in a world of Connecticut boarding schools, country clubs, and coming-out parties (they meant something different then), he grew up occupying and visiting a series of fine, well-run houses where pillows were correctly made and curtains correctly hung. But there is a casual, carefree side to his social set. As a child and adolescent, he was a natural at performing the sensual, everyday aspects of housekeeping at his family's shingle-style beach house in East Hampton, New York.

His large family still uses it all summer and on spring and fall weekends. Tom is unquestionably the cook. Whether it's he and a sister eating by themselves or a convivial party of ten or twenty, everything gets served up on

In 2001 Scheerer was commissioned to crisp up an elegantly proportioned Federal townhouse in Brooklyn Heights for a stylish young family. He designed a luminous living room for them, formal in scale but with a casual attitude. Its publication in *Elle Décor* coincided with a big uptick in Scheerer's business. His slacker life in Charleston was officially over and his busy frequent-flyer years began.

his grandmother's sprigged pink china. Afterward, guests are discouraged from helping clear dishes. The Scheerers leap up and do it.

The house has nine faded bedrooms, some with shared bathrooms. The kitchen's marble-topped center table has a jagged crack down the middle that's really a full-fledged break. It's been that way for decades. The back porch, the domain of the help in an earlier era, is tiny, but it serves as the family room. All the Scheerers cling to the unpretentious, makeshift way things used to be done in East Hampton. But the context has changed forever, and houses like theirs are now considered tear-downs. Most of their friends have sold and moved on. There's a showy new house next door with an ominous electronic gate. Its name is Dune Walk, but the Scheerers have never seen anyone come out of it on foot.

Scheerer's grandparents purchased their winsome beach house in 1945 from the writer Ring Lardner, along with Lardner's library of paperbacks and cast-off furniture. In those days, seasonal beach houses in this neck of the woods were passed along with their contents, in up-and-running condition so the family moving in wouldn't miss any summer fun. Taking stock of the dowdy, dark wood furniture, sagging chintz sofas, and old twin beds that came with the house, Scheerer's grandmother simply painted the stair treads coral pink, covered the walls in a geranium-blossom wallpaper, and painted all the furniture white, as it remains today. Over the years, a hat wall grew in a nook under the stairs. Scheerer admires this organic, seat-of-the-pants way of evoking freshness and happiness in a less than perfect situation, and he likes to reenact it or evoke its improvisational spirit.

After Scheerer completed his first major project—a spare and ravishing Brooklyn townhouse for a family of stylish Southern transplants—his work began appearing regularly in top design magazines, including *Elle Decor*, *House Beautiful*, and the vanished *House & Garden*. Then, about a dozen years ago, his career took a tropical turn when he was hired to decorate a hilltop house on Harbour Island in the Bahamas. Several other Harbour Island houses followed, including two potently atmospheric ones he made for himself. He found that the old East Hampton mode of expedient, spontaneous decorating worked particularly well in the Bahamas, where it's a huge effort and expense to obtain or maintain anything.

"It's my inner chintziness," he confesses. But it's also about his respect for an architecture's abiding personality. He'd rather work with a house more or less the way he finds it than expensively deracinate it with a gut renovation and impose his will on every square inch of it, as many prominent decorators do.

"Don't make too much trouble for yourself" is one of his mottos. "Live life now, rather than after a torturous renovation."

THE MODERN ASPECTS fueling Scheerer's decorating come from seeds planted three decades ago. In his mid-twenties, after a year of college in Switzerland and a string of pleasant, dead-end jobs, he enrolled in a five-year architecture program at the renowned Cooper Union in New York City. He thought he might like to design houses, and he already had the drawing skills. "As a child, I produced plans of houses and gardens as a way of explaining where I'd been, and I could dream up my own plans of places I wanted to go to," he says. "I must have picked this up from advertised floor plans of apartments in the *New York Times* or from cutaway views and deck plans in Cunard Line brochures."

But this was the 1980s, and in the classrooms of an avant-garde American architecture school, houses for actual people did not get much air time. Deconstructivism was finding its expression in architecture, and Scheerer's teachers were some of its best-known practitioners: architects Peter Eisenman, John Hedjuk, and Bernard Tschumi.

"At Cooper, we were expected to work on an entirely theoretical plane," Scheerer remembers. "It was a fascinating, cult-like education, but in the end, I didn't become indoctrinated. I'm too pragmatic, too much of a voluptuary. I don't have that kind of intellectual rigor. Compared to architecture, decorating is instant gratification."

Still, the Cooper Union years weren't for nothing. "I did drink a sip or two of the Kool-Aid," Scheerer says. "There's definitely a residue of it in my decorating."

It's there in the way he reads a house and corrects it by moving a doorway or raising a picture molding six inches. You can see it in his spare arrangements of objects. It's the invisible rigging behind his idolization of Saarinen tulip tables, Vernor Panton S chairs, Michael Thonet bentwood furniture, and other stellar precipitates of modernist thinking. It's in his stylized lines, his sense of proportion, his grasp of materials. It's in his avoidance of pretense in favor of rooms that work hard but look easy.

"I'm turned off by decorating when it becomes a religion," he says. "It's the superficiality and frivolity of decorating—as opposed to the dead serious word *design*—that actually appeals to me. You might say I go so far as to endorse a lack of rigor. But the fact is, even the superficial aspects of my decorating are backed up by an innate and also educated understanding of structural, aesthetic, and historical principles. In the end, it's all about being able to balance symmetry and asymmetry, deliberation and improvisation, harmony and dissonance. This is the nature of craft and art."

Another result of the Cooper Union education is that Scheerer prefers to let a house tell him what to do rather than the other way around. Its style, history, location, and floor plan dictate most of his design decisions. Seeing him walk through any house for the first time is revealing. Past the front door, he's as quiet as a wilderness scout for a few beats while he analyzes the space. Whether it's a decorating job or a friend's place, he quickly devises a detailed furniture plan as if reading it off a teleprompter and offers advice for architectural adaptations. If a painting crew is in the house's immediate future, he draws plans right on the walls. Though the decorative decisions come to him just as instantly, he doesn't pay attention to them until much further down the road, and they are the least important decisions, he insists. (If this contradicts his championing of the superficial, it's still the way he thinks.)

But of course, Scheerer dazzles in the paint, paper, and fabric arenas, too. Never harshly bright nor the least bit beige, his rooms instead sport fresh, clear colors in inspired combinations: Pink and cocoa brown. Aqua and heliotrope purple. Deep plum and saffron. Coral and grass green. It makes for a vibrant optimism.

In fabric, Scheerer gravitates toward generic and familiar workhorses. He loves cotton, linen, wool, dimity, and even candlewicking, an old-fangled embroidery of soft, thick thread on muslin. He simply ignores the existence of the thousands of heavily engineered fabrics available today. "I don't like fabrics that look like somebody went to too much trouble," he explains. "These complicated, overdesigned, overly elaborate fabrics—they're just not the texture of life that I like."

Though he claims he could make a perfectly successful house with no pattern at all, Scheerer keeps in his quiver fifteen or twenty old-fashioned prints, mostly American and French. They are among the airiest, prettiest, and most authentic-looking patterns anywhere, and he

In an uncharacteristic pose of relaxation, Scheerer sprawls on his upstairs sleeping porch on Harbour Island in the Bahamas. Originally a convent dating back to 1800, this coral stone building was the first of several houses he restored for himself and for clients on the island. Plywood daybeds were made on site. The rope chair, beachy driftwood lamp, and vase full of bougainvillea tell the story of the place. The gray and purple color scheme suits the tranquil, tropical mood.

uses them over and over. He saves fabric pieces, and if one gets discontinued, he'll usually re-create it, often in zingier colors. Indian fabrics have always held a special attraction for him, and he's been known to make curtains, pillows, and bed hangings out of inexpensive Indian print bedspreads for even the worldliest clients.

Whether it's fabrics or bentwood chairs, using the same elements over and over is never a problem for Scheerer. He doesn't chase the new. Many decorators and their clients want fireworks. But Scheerer doesn't try to bowl you over with extreme novelty or extreme anything. He's not easily impressed, and he's not terribly interested in impressing people. He's the decorator for the long haul, the one who can compose a great-looking room that you never want to leave. He knows comforting, useful things like where to put a table, a light switch, a television, and a chair. It's generally subliminal, but in a Scheerer house you'll always feel that, despite all the worrisome evidence outside, the universe remains on course.

Nevertheless, if you're one of the high arbiters of American style who look at reams of contemporary decorating images every day, Scheerer's rooms just might stop you in your tracks. In late 2010, that's what happened to Stephen Drucker while planning a spring issue of *Town & Country*.

"The first time I was handed a scouting photograph of the Lyford Cay Club's living room—a bad snapshot— I looked up and said, 'This is a room that's going to be remembered,'" Drucker recalls. "It was the first time I'd said that in years. It was like Nancy Lancaster's yellow room or Billy Baldwin's chocolate brown studio apartment. It had such spirit, such scale."

Seventeen-foot-tall fantasy palm trees had been stenciled in ivory on the vast room's chocolate brown grasscloth-covered walls. Pink and green islands of upholstered furniture floated completely naturally. When Drucker ran photographs of the club in the April 2011 issue, Scheerer's career got a big bump up. Everyone saw that he was capable of doing anything he wanted with his rare and idiosyncratic touch—even something he'd never done before.

"There's nothing harder than redecorating a club," Drucker continues. "You've got all these people, half of whom want nothing to change. No two people agree on taste, and every member has a right to be heard. You have to have Tom's extreme confidence to get such privileged people to follow you. And of course, he delivered. In refreshing the club, he made it new but it didn't lose the *it* of it. That's not easy."

FROM HIS PARK AVENUE OFFICE, a cozy aerie overlooking rooftops and water towers in the Flatiron District, Scheerer continues to design six or seven houses a year. For himself, he continues to love seasonal houses used in summer or winter and then boarded up. Recently, he put the crowning touches on an 1820s Maine farmhouse he owns with one of his sisters. When the curtain goes down on the East Hampton house and the Scheerers surrender to reality and sell it, he wants there to be a magical new setting where the family can convene. Life will continue in Maine. The new owners of the East Hampton house will likely let the local fire department set fire to it for practice before clearing away the rubble to make way for another supersized house, but he won't be watching. He'll be in Maine, collecting stones, making wonderful things to eat, or watching the sun come up over distant islands.

In the following pages, photographs of some recent Scheerer projects fall into three sections: City, Country, and Tropics. There's a great deal to learn from each one about color, pattern, comfort, arranging a room, running a house, and most important, making it all feel natural and effortless. It's also a logical and languorous way to look at interiors in which a strong, appropriate sense of place is so vivid. Think of it as travel. Scheerer's houses are marvelous destinations and he is good company and an endlessly fascinating guide.

Scheerer's Manhattan office is both a design laboratory and a repository for his stuff. He bought the seventeenth-century Flemish ebonized kas, or Dutch cupboard, in the early 1980s at Christie's and so far has dragged it from New York to Charleston to the Bahamas and back. Right now, it's full of his collection of antique fabric remnants and documents. The 1970s vintage faux-tortoiseshell screens have now been installed in the dining room of the Piping Rock Club on Long Island. Here they're mounted with staghorn ferns, one of his favorite indoor plants. The paintings and mixed-media collages are his own. He makes them in his apartment before the sun rises.

City

Propriety with Aplomb

SCHEERER IS BRILLIANT AT FINDING WAYS TO make decorating schemes that are traditional but also bursting with energy and imagination. The need for propriety in a house never weighs him down. He grew up with it and knows exactly which rules can flex and which ones never will. In this old-fashioned Brooklyn Heights apartment created for a young banker, his wife, and their children, even the gravely beautiful rooms are nonchalant, and the least promising spaces have been transformed into showstoppers.

"This couple and I have always communicated in shorthand," says Scheerer, who decorated two previous Brooklyn apartments for them. "No need to convince *them* that a red library works. This library was their third red room in three consecutive apartments!"

If all foyers need to be arranged for practicality with a warmly lit table, a mirror, a tray for mail, a dish for keys, and a chair for boot removal, they also ask for a dash of theater—something that sets the tone for the rest of the house. For this featureless entry, Scheerer convinced the clients to invest in a fine Regency pier table that suits the stature of the apartment. He flanked it with two Baldwin slipper chairs in coral pink and created interest with an otherworldly grisaille scenic paper above the wainscoting.

It's his favorite Zuber panorama: Paysage Italien. You almost hear the leaves rustling. "I always go back to this one. It's landscape painting without human figures or architecture," he says. As an improvisation, he used leftover scraps of it to cover two pink-lined lampshades for a pair of sconces—a dreamy detail with a touch of surreal whimsy.

Wallpaper long on personality was Scheerer's salvation again in what was originally a windowless corridor too narrow even for hanging pictures. He turned it into the most vivacious spot in the house by covering its walls in Lyford Trellis, a favorite paper that he rescued from oblivion, here in bracing coral, red, and cream. "It has a Brighton Pavilion kind of gaiety," he says. A soldier's course of mirrors brings in light from bedrooms along the corridor. The shell-backed chair placed at the terminus was design manna, nicely seized upon. "It's a perfect fit, and there's a level of realness to it—it came from the wife's grandmother," says Scheerer, always attuned to matters of authenticity.

The family entertains often, but they also use their dining room when they're alone because it's so easygoing. All decorators say their rooms are timeless, but this one actually is. Nothing trendy has been allowed in. The intimate round table was found on the Internet. It arrived with a charming surprise: an old Parish-Hadley label on the bottom. Scheerer added two shepherd's crook armchairs to the client's cache of splat-back chairs and pulled these around the table, which also backs up to an English Regency sofa upholstered in plush mohair. This is aristocratic décor at its most relaxed and appealing. It's a lot of brown wood, but it isn't boring. Very little matches, yet it's all part of the same burnished mood.

"This is not a stage set for a properly lived life. It's real," Scheerer says. "As long as people don't take their nice things too seriously, the nice things work."

OPPOSITE Picturesque grisaille wallpaper panels and a fine William IV pier table set a lush, stately tone in a Brooklyn Heights apartment. Classic and correct in their petite proportions, the coral slipper chairs come from a Connecticut house decorated by the late Billy Baldwin. **OVERLEAF, LEFT** A shell-backed English hall chair is posed against Scheerer's signature Lyford Trellis wallpaper, the irresistible Chinese Chippendale pattern he revived and reprinted with Quadrille. The leopard-patterned carpet is a durable, chic choice for the high traffic of family life. **OVERLEAF, RIGHT** A series of formally spaced full-length mirrors and overhead drum shades reinforce the drama in a narrow hallway.

OPPOSITE In a feminine, pale blue bedroom, the client's grandmother's dresser was painted and decoupaged with photocopies of the flowery fabric used elsewhere in the room—one of Scheerer's favorite bangs for the buck. **ABOVE** The old-fashioned skirted dressing table sets off a vintage Danish mirror and a 1950s Saarinen taboret. The ethereal winter landscapes are by Kathryn Lynch.

ABOVE Scheerer gave the living room an informal airiness. Walls are covered in handmade bark-paper rectangles, which add subtle texture. He designed a handsome, durable coffee table of antique Coromandel panels and patinated bronze. **RIGHT** Chinese temple figures line up on the mantelpiece. **FAR RIGHT** Scheerer made use of a corner, filling it with a festive Turkish-style banquette for extra seating. Above the Suzani-patterned banquette, the landscape is by Stephen Hannock and the large figure painting is by Judy Wilson.

PROPRIETY WITH APLOMB . 25

ABOVE LEFT An English Regency sideboard holds the bar and a pair of silvered-brass Indian candlesticks made into attenuated lamps. In the corner, a potted fiddle leaf fig tree adds scale. **TOP RIGHT** The table is set for a weeknight family dinner with fringed napkins and a casual arrangement of sunflowers. **ABOVE RIGHT** Scheerer brought in leather-covered shepherd's crook chairs to mix with the owners' collection of Queen Anne–style dining chairs. **OPPOSITE** To further vary seating options, the antique pedestal table is pulled up to a graceful nineteenth-century English settee. Scheerer resized and reused a beautifully worn Oushak carpet from the clients' previous apartment, which he also decorated. **OVERLEAF** Most of the furnishings in the library, with its warm and welcoming red-glazed walls, are from the couple's previous apartment. Scheerer re-covered their St. Thomas sofa in a cocoa linen velvet and resized mahogany and scorched-bamboo bookcases. The midcentury chairs in blue linen were a new purchase, however, and Scheerer designed the tufted, leather-topped ottoman coffee table for the room.

New Wave in Brooklyn Heights

In the 1950s and '60s, the writer Truman Capote lived in a townhouse apartment in Brooklyn Heights that he decorated himself, combining his bohemian collections with conventional Victorian furnishings. Capote allowed these two strains of his character—the bohemian artist and the respectable Southerner—to coexist in a way that was lively and a touch loony. Scheerer has always loved that dichotomous look. "Sometimes the best decorators aren't decorators at all—they're people with ideas," he says.

It was, in part, Capote's Brooklyn interlude that was on Scheerer's mind when he reconceived this 1820s Greek Revival townhouse in the same neighborhood for a young family. But the project also made him think about all the people who'd lived there and left their marks on the house for nearly two hundred years. Scheerer, who hates to push a house too far out of character, wanted to keep some of those historical layers, and even invented a few of them. He sees his young clients as the latest in the long parade of Brooklyn immigrants. "Who knew the current wave would be hedgies with a predisposition for midcentury Danish furniture?" he asks wryly.

A purist would have taken the house back to its Greek Revival origins. But Scheerer prefers an American storyline here. "I like the almost Gothic-y elements, like the front door," he says. "And I appreciate those exuberant, confectionary marble mantelpieces. I imagine they were added after the turn of the century by an Italian family, possibly in the funeral monument business!"

After a renovation that included redoing seven bathrooms and adding a kitchen, he papered the stair hall in a document print from the year the house was built. He recolored the early-nineteenth-century Ada Harris pattern in a slighty kooky palette of pink, coral, yellow, and brown that's meant to look like it came with the house. Scheerer notes that it's very much in sync with the bentwood console table. And though that table works with historical precision in this instance, Scheerer can usually find a place for Michael Thonet's late-nineteenth-century excursions into elegant, curlicued furniture in any sort of house. "It has joyous buoyancy," Scheerer says of all bentwood. "I never get tired of it. Bentwood is a lyric note you can pull out of your pocket when you need it, and it contrasts beautifully with the hard edges that seem to be everywhere."

Scheerer kept the living room's furniture spare and understated on purpose, letting fourteen-foot ceilings and ornate moldings speak for themselves. After removing a pair of chandeliers from the double parlor—he dislikes most chandeliers for their fanciness and the aqueous haze of their light—he put up large rice-paper lanterns by Isamu Noguchi. "I love them," he says. "It's like hanging the moon." He designed the modernist ottoman that floats mid-room on the chicken wire–patterned carpet, and in the adjacent parlor, carefully balanced with this one, he composed a Magritte-ish vignette in which a cloudlike puff of a sofa sits lightly beneath a painting of clouds. "City houses," Scheerer says, "can be more cerebral than country houses."

In the master bedroom, he used an especially tall four-poster bed to take advantage of the room's scale and height. Its white Indian cutwork bedspread is Scheerer's fresher, more exotic substitute for conventional matelassé bedding. But the most singular object in the room is the wonderfully animated Jacques Adnet silent valet, a profusion of right angles made of reedy bamboo. It stands under a long-legged flower drawing by Hugo Guinness, a London-born artist who lives in the neighborhood.

"It's like a praying mantis," says Scheerer. "It brings the room to life. Most clients would not understand it, but these clients saw it as a work of art and consequently they never put anything on it. The irony of this valet is that it really is best left alone."

OPPOSITE In a Brooklyn Heights townhouse for a young couple, Scheerer used a fine example of his beloved bentwood furniture—in this case, a curlicued Austrian console table—to mark the entry with a jaunty Ragtime flavor. The wallpaper is a historic reproduction of the early-nineteenth-century Ada Harris pattern by Adelphi Paper Hangings but recolored by Scheerer.

TOP LEFT The clients' collection of vintage American pottery is displayed throughout the house. **TOP RIGHT** Ebullient carving ornaments the double parlor's Carrara marble mantelpieces. **ABOVE** Arts & Crafts sunflower tiles, later additions to the original house, decorate the hearth slab. **OPPOSITE** In the living room, sprouting coconut palms bring Dr. Seuss-like energy to the room. A Frits Henningsen wing chair speaks to the clients' love of sleek Danish modern design. The large Noguchi paper globe with a lunar spirit is one of a pair—the other side of the double parlor features its mate.

OPPOSITE Slipcovered in pale blue, John Derian's Dromedary sofa takes on a surreal, ghostly presence, an effect that's heightened by Richard Misrach's cloud photograph. Scheeer designed amusing Gothic-style radiator enclosures with stone tops. **ABOVE** Scheerer stripped the service wing down to its brick walls and installed a slick, modern kitchen by Bulthaup. The inverted T of the stainless-steel stove hood is bold, incidental sculpture. Reclaimed chestnut floors are meant to look original to the house. Bentwood chairs are easily moved to the dining room when needed.

OPPOSITE The sitting room walls are covered in a highly textured, deep brown grasscloth. To corral books, Scheerer installed his trademark wall-hung midcentury-style boxes. The Robert Motherwell lithograph adds graphic punctuation. **ABOVE** Scheerer designed the vaulted passageway that connects the sitting room to the master bedroom. A Hans Wegner armchair shares the sitting room with an upholstered chair covered in Quadrille's Persepolis print in fresh colors: aqua, white, and brown.

ABOVE LEFT Regarded as a fine sculpture by Scheerer and his clients, a Jacques Adnet silent valet made of bamboo, brass, and leather stands beneath a faux-naïf flower drawing by Hugo Guinness. **TOP RIGHT** Ferns and leaves from the townhouse garden make a simple, modern arrangement. **ABOVE RIGHT** Upstairs doors were made to match the Gothic detailing of the front door. **OPPOSITE** In the master bedroom, the mood reflects the lean airiness of the rooms downstairs, but with a touch more femininity. Pale blue walls shimmer in high-gloss paint. The monumental reproduction American four-poster bed was made to fit the room. The personable Frits Henningsen wing chair is covered in a seafoam midcentury-style fabric.

Art and Decorating

Sometimes clients rely on Scheerer to guide them in buying art for their houses. Yet he's always happy when they come to him with their own points of view—or better still—with interesting collections they've amassed. "People confident in their own tastes are easy to work with," he says. "Their interest and pleasure in a collection is often a clear guide for the decorating." In the case of this Manhattan apartment overlooking a sweep of Central Park, he was thrilled to find clients with several quirky collections they'd assembled passionately and on their own. Within their trove of sculptures are some yawning babies' heads in terra-cotta and several sleeping figures in plaster.

In addition to decorating the apartment, Scheerer transformed it by rearranging the art. "Placement is everything," he says. "People tend to look at their collections either chronologically or historically. But when you break that cycle, a house can take a big leap forward. What I try for is an overall feeling of balance but with unexpected juxtapositions."

The entrance hall is his tour de force. To give the apartment a warm and welcoming core, Scheerer covered the walls in grasscloth stenciled in a Mughal pattern—his grown-up version of hanging an Indian bedspread on a dorm room wall. He turned existing sconces into sexy exclamation points with the addition of lampshades covered in pleated Indian print scarves; they're lined in pink silk and encircled with bordello fringe. He credits the late, great Renzo Mongiardino for inspiring this vignette. A sunflower photograph by Adam Fuss leans casually against a 1970s Venetian-style mirror, while Isabel McIlvain's white marble sculpture of a recumbent woman is tucked under the modern Chinese console, adding strangeness and life. "The sculpture is already provocative on its own, but to find an obese, naked woman sleeping it off underneath the front hall table, it's all the more interesting," Scheerer says. Georgian chairs stand sentry in a wonderful copy of their original tattered upholstery. Scheerer had mailed off scraps of the old crewelwork to a friend's factory in India, which reproduced it handily.

With Scheerer on board, the couple hoped to turn their living room into an active part of the house rather than a room peered into and passed by. To that end, he designed a modernist chaise for reading and napping and laid it with a vibrant plaid Missoni blanket that warms the room like a bonfire. A photograph of Tupperware by artist Richard Caldicott hangs over it. The space feels playful, more like some sublime version of a kid's room than a fancy living room. Scheerer also used one of his favorite trompe l'oeil devices: he covered the walls in bark paper bought at an art supply store, the handmade sheets creamy and irregular. "If you want to do a beige or white room without it being too cool or lifeless, it's a great trick," he says. "It has a vague 1930s air when put up in squares, or if you put it up in horizontal rectangles, it feels like neoclassical stonework." It also hides rehanging marks well—a bonus for collectors who like to move art around.

On the other side of the living room, he played with ideas about symmetry and asymmetry. The dynamic arrangement of flaxen furniture includes six wildly different seating pieces, each offering its own special quality and comfort. The patterned carpet by Allegra Hicks—a Scheerer favorite—is an adaptation of something Picasso-esque and African, and it brings with it the dynamism of its undulating forms. Scheerer didn't forget to weave art into the glamour. A purple photograph of silhouetted leaves by Susan Derges hangs over the snappy slipper chair, and an anonymous bronze female nude stands in the window like a compelling idol over the deep, luxurious Chesterfield sofa.

OPPOSITE In a Manhattan apartment where art is liberally woven into the atmosphere, Scheerer rehung the client's collection of Robert Kulicke paintings in period frames around an antique Venetian mirror.

ABOVE AND RIGHT The warm, slightly nightclubby entry is done up in hippie deluxe style. Yellow silk grasscloth walls were stenciled with Indian patterns by Brian Leaver. Scheerer made fringed shades for the sconces and added the 1970s mirror, where family snapshots get wedged in the corners. A sculpture of a sleeping woman by Isabel McIlvain is casually tucked under the contemporary Chinese lacquered console table. The sunflower photograph is by Adam Fuss.

LEFT The living room's playful spirit comes from its informal furnishings, art arrangements, and loose color scheme. Scheerer designed the modernist daybed and dressed it with a plaid Missoni throw. The squiggly plum and saffron kilim was designed by Allegra Hicks for Christopher Farr. **ABOVE, CLOCKWISE FROM TOP LEFT** Scheerer, who has always loved spheres and circles, arranged metal finials and floats as found sculptures on the mantelpiece; ceramic babies' heads by Isabel McIlvain are strewn among books; a midcentury chrome and suede taboret poses under a winter landscape photograph by Elger Esser; the regal bronze figure was picked up at auction for $100. **OVERLEAF** The animated 1950s chair in the foreground links the more playful side of the living room with this, its slightly dressier zone. At almost ten feet long, Scheerer's enormous modernist version of a Chesterfield sofa is upholstered in a cocoa mohair velvet for sumptuous comfort. The off-the-rack glass and steel coffee table is a reproduction of the one Mies van der Rohe designed in 1929 for the Barcelona Pavilion. **PAGES 48–49** Pierce Allen Architects designed the library's casework for an earlier decorating scheme. The clients' own Heriz rug dictated the room's orange and blue palette. Scheerer designed the cozy upholstered furniture as well as the linen and silk "burlap" Roman shades, flounced to add soft curves to the room.

City Kids

IT'S THE RARE CHILD WHO GROWS UP KNOWING OR caring what big-time decorating looks like, never mind what it feels like to live with. But Scheerer encountered a couple of young decorating fans when he was asked to update their bedrooms in a Manhattan apartment owned by their indulgent parents.

The apartment has a rich history of high-style decoration. Over the years, exceptional designers have worked on its rooms, including Colfax & Fowler, known for its eclectic English and French schemes. Scheerer saw his role as one who could bring a bit of modernism to a task that is too often met with puerile emblems and themes. No *Babes in Toyland* for him! He aimed for rooms sophisticated enough to carry the children into adulthood, with the idea that in coming years, they'd return home as guests.

In the boy's bedroom, he covered the existing boiserie in high-gloss white marine paint to give it modern gleam, then filled the room with a mix of inventions, antiques, and mass-market pieces. "Thereç's nothing worse than having everything in a room be at the same level of quality," he says. "I've always liked the contrast of everyday things with rare or refined ones. In a strange way, too much fancy furniture in one place devalues the good stuff."

The boy's magnificent four-poster was a daunting undertaking. It was inspired in part by a Horst photograph of a towering bed belonging to the late Baron Philippe de Rothschild, who is said to have conducted most of his life in bed. Scheerer designed this one as a campaign bed and had it made out of brass fittings, blackened steel tubing, and channel-quilted grasscloth panels. "Fitting all the small parts together was a high-wire act," he says. "After pulling off such a formidable bed, it was nice to fall back on a generic Parsons table desk that came with a click off the Internet."

The girl's bedroom is softer and sweeter. "It's like being inside a wedding cake," he says. He emphasized its French paneling by glazing it in various hues of robin's-egg blue. The bed's lavender linen headboard has a fanciful shape and the purple cashmere blanket folded at the foot adds a luxurious band of color. The lavender and robin's-egg blue palette is one that Scheerer finds fresh and spirited, and he uses it often.

The ensuite bathrooms were treated to two of Scheerer's favorite wallpapers. The boy's has a black-and-white snowflake print designed and often used by dandy and photographer Cecil Beaton as a portrait background. The girl's is jazzed up with Lyford Trellis, a Chinoiserie bamboo lattice print in ethereal robin's-egg blue.

This wallpaper is Scheerer's most exuberant signature. He likes it in colors tame and wild, and he's able to find a place for it in remarkably different settings. It always adds character, high spirits, and vintage charm. Twenty years ago he found an old roll of it in the back of his family's linen closet in East Hampton. It had been on the walls in his grandmother's sunroom when Scheerer was a child, but the one roll was all that remained. The company had stopped making it.

Fiercely nostalgic for beautiful lost and discontinued items, Scheerer had this fanciful and highly decorative pattern copied in startling new colors. It's now a bestseller.

OPPOSITE For a boy's bedroom in New York City, Scheerer made a double-sided hemisphere map that turns on a string. The nineteenth-century étagère was purchased at auction. The bronze rhinoceros was a gift from the boy's parents.

ABOVE The boy's bathroom is papered in a Cecil Beaton design, a wallpaper reproduced for Scheerer by Quadrille. Scheerer designed the triangular, mirror-backed nickel sconces.
RIGHT Scheerer dreamed up and assembled the brass and steel four-poster bed from standard bar-rail tubing and connectors. Overscaled ceramic lamps are vintage. The Parson's desk at the window is from West Elm. Wembly club chairs from Ballard Design are covered in a graphic distillation of a classic French print made for Scheerer in black and white by Quadrille.

OPPOSITE In the girl's bedroom the boiserie is more ornate than in her brother's room, and Scheerer picked out its carving with three shades of robin's-egg blue glazing. Bedside lamps are 1960s vintage finds from the Dixie Highway in West Palm Beach. A Louis XVI armchair—one of a pair—is covered in printed linen reminiscent of a Rorschach test. Near the window are porcelain botanical flowers mounted in a shadow box. **ABOVE** The color scheme of lilac and robin's-egg blue gives the room a soft buzz of electricity. A shaped headboard upholstered in coarse lilac linen heightens the feminine mood. **OVERLEAF, LEFT** The girl's sitting area is a luxurious nook with a John Derian sofa, a lacquered-cube coffee table, and a Baldwin slipper chair upholstered in Carolina Irving's Andaluz. **OVERLEAF, RIGHT** In the ensuite bath, Scheerer used his Lyford Trellis wallpaper in robin's-egg blue and white, ethereal colors that give its intricate bamboo fretwork a lacy charm. Scheerer put new shades on existing shell sconces, had them rewired, and let them be.

Patrician Polish

Appropriateness is Tom Scheerer's fundamental watchword. He always decorates to suit the architecture and the setting. His houses believably reflect the people who live in them and are not used to express false aspirations or fantasies. His work may be dynamic, playful, and patently chic, but it is also, to a degree, circumspect. He's not the sort of decorator whose first instinct is to create a full-dress Moroccan screening room for a Los Angeles film executive, nor has he fashioned Manhattan financiers' homes to look like those of British aristocrats.

Though he avoids pretense and fanciness as a rule, he knows there are instances when a decorous elegance is called for. This apartment on Manhattan's Upper East Side is one of them. The couple hails from venerable European and American backgrounds. The dukes, duchesses, prime ministers, and captains of industry staring out of small picture frames on their tabletops are, in fact, their close relatives.

Scheerer composed for them a dynamic living room with a quietly grand touch. Walls are a buoyant yellow, but otherwise he steered clear of bright color. "The room is architecturally perfect, with four magnificent north-facing windows," he says. "There wasn't a need to distract with color." He made good use of the family furniture, a confluence of English and French pieces that includes two bergères à la reine and a Louis XVI child's chair.

The rest of the furnishings he acquired for the space, arranging everything with "deliberate English haphazardness," he says, so it would feel relaxed and engagingly salon-like. He chose Cogolin straw carpeting for much the same reason—it takes the pall of fanciness off the room. It's a special Provençal brand with varied color and texture, and one of its beauties is the visible seaming, which tells how it was made—by hand and on small looms. Scheerer loves exactly this kind of artisanal, small-batch product that entails a craft and has lost none of its quirky integrity over the years.

In the dining room, a previous decorator had painted the walls in bold persimmon. Scheerer liked the rich color and the crosshatched glazing with visible brushwork, so he kept it. But a nineteenth-century sporting painting was deemed too predictable, so he and the homeowners embarked on a program of modern art collecting, which led to the purchase of four black-and-white photographs by Stephen Inggs. These edgier pictures were framed simply and hung together over a Louis XVI–style bench. The gold-tooled leather Régence dining chairs, on the other hand, were chosen for their patina. They add a wonderful feeling of depth and history, especially in juxtaposition to the minimal steel and zebrawood dining table of Scheerer's design. A contemporary kilim by Allegra Hicks in deep plum and saffron adds one more jolt of pattern and modern zap.

At the far end of the apartment, Scheerer pulled off one of his signature feats: an intimate, old-fashioned room that manages to be cozily familiar and chic at once. It's a red-trimmed library that also serves as an office for the lady of the house. Scheerer designed the elegant, attenuated desk with a saddle-leather top on brass sawhorses. But the real pizzazz comes from a pair of inexpensive catalogue staples: for desk seating, Scheerer cheekily chose two injection-molded plastic S chairs suffused with aerodynamic charm, throwaway sexiness, and even a design pedigree—their pioneering prototype was coined in 1967 by Vernor Panton. These swooping, futuristic beauties have long been in Scheerer's bag of tricks—they're one of his weapons to ward off stuffiness.

"The Panton chairs, desk, and Mies ottoman bring the whole thing into the twentieth century," says Scheerer. But some things never change, and Scheerer treasures those bits, too: the "brutalist" pottery made by the homeowners' sons when they were young, family pictures tucked here and there, and a well-used guitar propped against the mantelpiece.

OPPOSITE Scheerer inherited the dining room's orange glazed walls from a previous decorator. It was the only element of the earlier décor that he kept, however. The clients wanted to jazz up the apartment, so he guided them to replace a massive nineteenth-century painting of hunting dogs with a grid of minimally framed modern photographs.

PRECEDING PAGES The living room's seemingly casual arrangement of furniture is actually highly calibrated for a dynamic balance. Its color scheme is relaxed and neutral with accents of blue, green, and brown. The antique chairs come from the owners' families; Scheerer added the slipper chairs, sofa, and daybed. On sunny yellow walls, three Alex Katz paintings are hung in a column for an up-to-date punch. **ABOVE** Scheerer likes color to flow harmoniously from room to room, as in this view from the yellow living room into the orange dining room. **OPPOSITE** A Donald Baechler drawing of tulips hangs above the dining room's Directoire commode. On its dark marble top, the group of antique porcelain artists' palettes was assembled by Scheerer, who made the Plexiglas box to house them.

ABOVE The most personal room in the apartment is a cozy library that the wife uses as her office. The armchairs are upholstered in a vermicelli-quilted, traditional French botanical print, Jardin des Plantes, by Charles Burger. Two sinuous Panton chairs are pulled up to a brass and leather sawhorse desk that Scheerer designed. **OPPOSITE** A Mies van der Rohe Barcelona ottoman is both coffee table and footstool for seating around the fireplace. Scheerer covered the walls in brown grasscloth that has been stenciled with a Mughal-style print.

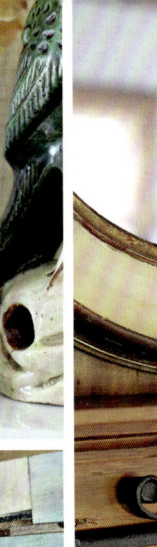

Country

Farmhouse Redux

ARCHITECTURALLY, THE ORIGINAL INTERIOR OF this eighteenth-century homestead abutting ancient Long Island potato fields has the feeling of a half-timbered Normandy farmhouse. This is a happy coincidence, because the owners inherited some good, comfortable French furniture from their respective parents and it looks believable here.

"In America, French decorating usually comes across as false, affected, or random," Scheerer says. "But here it happened naturally and the architecture was a natural fit." He re-covered the family furniture and jazzed up the atmosphere with new art, shapely vintage finds, catalogue furnishings, energizing colors, and lots of crazy, chic pattern.

Scheerer's foremost idea was to let the rustic architectural elements engender the decorative ones. Taking one look at a sitting room's emphatic rectilinear beams and joists, he got the idea for a round braided rug—and not an Early American–style braided rug, that dowdy cliché of country decor. Instead he designed a fantastically bold whirlpool of a rug with crisp white and brown concentric circles. It almost churns the room.

"The sharp contrast between the bands of the braided rug and the rectilinear beams of a similar scale tell a powerful story about structure," he says. "It's kinetic, strong, jarring, and logical, all at the same time." While the circular shape acts like extended arms, a warm invitation to gather round, the dynamic pattern keeps the traditional arrangement of a sofa and fauteuils from feeling the least bit sedate.

Scheerer, in fact, gave every room its own dose of mod energy. In the dining room, he gains calligraphic momentum by showing off the beaky profiles of birds in Swedish naturalist prints next to spouted creamware pitchers stored in a painted cupboard.

In the main living room, he kept in mind that houseguests come and go often. The boys and their friends drift in and out. Furniture arrangements are somewhat free-form to accommodate different activities and age groups. Worked into the mix are two sinuous midcentury wing chairs re-covered in crewelwork, an Early American salute.

Scheerer is not hesitant to wade into the realm of uber-traditional decorating when it seems right, and anyway, he always manages to come up with a fresh execution that adds new layers of meaning. In a guest bedroom, he allowed himself to be as French as French can be by covering the walls and chairs in a red eighteenth-century document toile de Jouy called Lafayette—his favorite toile.

"I like its Franco-American historical value. It depicts Native Americans, palm trees, and guns rather than twee Fragonard-esque shepherdesses," he says. The room formerly had a Louis XV–style upholstered headboard, which he nixed in favor of a more modern rope-wrapped one from a catalogue.

On the back porch, where the family tends to gather, Scheerer introduced a set of mixed-vintage rattan pole furniture and covered its cushions in deep purple canvas with a navy welt. This big taste of unmitigated purple is unexpected, to say the least. But in Scheerer's mind, it's absolutely correct.

"Purple is an often overlooked color," he says. "It doesn't get dirty like white or beige, so the cushions last twenty years. It's a wonderful foil for green. It's also a color that's ever present in nature. Just look at the paintings of the Impressionists—the shadows are always purple."

OPPOSITE In a casual sitting room, a braided-wool whirlpool rug in crisp brown and white counterbalances the rectilinear beams of the ceiling and walls. The sofa is covered in brown-and-white mattress ticking and the loose, airy floral print on its pillows is one of Scheerer's favorites: Secret Garden by Raoul Textiles. Above the sofa are two framed pages of the original deed to the house. The sheared-flokati ottoman adds softness and interrupts the whirling motion of the carpet. **OVERLEAF** The living room's mix of fabrics includes a vermicelli-quilted Muriel Brandolini paisley print on the sofa. Sofa pillows are made from a green challis shawl and purple pick-stitch cotton by Pierre Frey. The Americana crewelwork covering the wing chairs was made in India.

ABOVE AND OPPOSITE The dining room's sunny wall color is Pratt & Lambert's Burnt Sage, a Scheerer favorite with a misleading name—it's really the color of ripe mango. The bird prints are from a reproduction of a folio by Olof Rudbeck, an eighteenth-century Swedish naturalist. The table and chairs are family furniture. Scheerer amassed the collection of white pitchers for the rustic cabinet.

PRECEDING PAGES Scheerer added a bay window to flood the kitchen with natural light and create a sitting area, the centerpiece of which is a magenta burlap ottoman. The cork floor was stained with stripes for graphic interest and to suggest wide wooden planks. French bistro chairs surrounding the long breakfast table lend sinuous flair. **RIGHT** In this family room, the walls are covered with a Nobilis paper that mimics blond wood paneling—a trompe l'oeil trick that Scheerer loves for its economy, effectiveness, and ease; here the boards run horizontally for a modern feeling. The sofa, chair, and bench are covered in the same happy vintage print fabric. Side tables are old ceramic whiskey barrels.

ABOVE In the distaff master bath, sloped walls and a dormer are covered in striped cotton. Vintage Venetian glass dressing table lamps and a tilting mirror make an elegant composition. Scheerer designed the vanity with feminine curves. **OPPOSITE** The walls in a downstairs powder room are upholstered in The Aviary, an American toile from Schumacher that camouflages the awkward shape of the room, originally a pantry that Scheerer repurposed.

ABOVE Scheerer modernized the owners' old-fashioned French twin beds by upholstering their head- and footboards in grasscloth. He made cheery café curtains for the window behind a two-tiered oak and cane nightstand; he doesn't like long curtains falling behind furniture. **OPPOSITE** In another bedroom, Scheerer covered walls and a chair in Lafayette, a narrative Americana document toile by Charles Burger. The rope headboard came with a click on the Internet. Scheerer, who occasionally makes art for his clients, cut out each paper butterfly by hand to create the whimsical shadow box above the bed. **OVERLEAF** A covered porch is furnished with vintage rattan furniture topped by purple Sunbrella cushions piped in blue. French park chairs are pulled up to a custom teak table with a slate top. The hooded wicker basket chair was a gift from the owner's mother.

American Splendor

BUILT IN THE TRADITION OF GRAND RHODE Island summer cottages, this new house sprawls across a ravishing parcel at the edge of Watch Hill, an old line summer playground awash in its New England heritage. The windows and terraces overlook a long sweep of dune, a tidal pond, and Block Island Sound.

Due to the extensive scope of the project, the building process was long and arduous. At the finish, the homeowners hoped that the architecture might carry the day and they made only timid forays into decorating. But their efforts fell flat. So they called on Scheerer. He knew right away that the vast spaces needed a strong hand and bold strokes. English country houses immediately came to mind, and from there his thoughts segued to the late English decorator David Hicks and his wonderful wallpaper The Vase.

"It has a fancy damask quality but at the same time a lively informality," Scheerer says. "It looks a bit like a wax-resist batik print. Hicks used it in a similarly scaled front hall to domesticate a very grand country house." Custom printed in a clear marine blue to celebrate the ocean-side setting, Scheerer's version of this eternally fresh wallpaper turned the imposing two-story hall into a much jollier affair.

Besides the paradigm of English county house style, Scheerer found a couple of American historical themes inherent in the setting. Ferreting out themes and storylines in a house is his standard operating procedure because they give personality and definition to any project and keep the hundreds of decorating decisions from being random and meaningless. Watch Hill is just off the Pequod Trail, and the clients had a magnificent bust of a Rhode Island chieftain. Scheerer found a perch for him in the hallway. He later purchased a terra-cotta plaque depicting another local chieftain and installed it on the stair landing below the clients' collection of antique maps, which are suspended from brass rails as if in a Grand Tour picture gallery.

In the living room, the Chinoiserie screens, coffee table, and primitive paintings of clipper ships reflect the history of Providence and Newport, both active ports on the old China trade route. For texture and character, Scheerer covered the walls in grasscloth. The room breathes in light and air, and he enhanced this clean brightness by upholstering a sofa and two chairs in horizontally striped linen with a sunny, nautical vibe. The stylized chintz covering other chairs and pillows has a taupe ground with white camellias and dark blue leaves, and it's one of Scheerer's favorites.

"It's a strange, unexpected colorway of a distinctly American-style chintz," he says. "I like to think it recalls Dorothy Draper at the Greenbrier."

The living room is also home to a lot of vintage Bar Harbor wicker furniture in various shapes. "We had to knock the fanciness out of the house and keep on doing it!" Scheerer says. Wicker is one of his summer-house tricks for accomplishing just that.

The coloring and spirit of the Hicks wallpaper continues in the kitchen and breakfast room, where Scheerer covered large expanses of wall in Cuban tiles in a graphic blue-and-white daisy pattern. "When I use tile in a kitchen I think of it as wallpaper and like to use it everywhere, not just as a backsplash," he says. The kitchen opens into an upbeat family room. There, the seat cushions on a bright blue corduroy sofa, its color brisk as a salute, sport paisley-patterned slipcovers that can be washed and eventually replaced without re-covering the whole sofa. They give the room a casual look.

As Billy Baldwin wisely wrote, "Nothing is interesting unless it's personal." In this house, the dining room has its roots in a cultural history that Scheerer and the clients share. Friendships between their families go back several generations.

"The dining room was inspired by my family's summer dining room in East Hampton," Scheerer says. "It had bad brown furniture that my grandmother freshened with white paint. There was and still is an overall blue and white scheme. Her sunroom had the progenitor of the Lyford Trellis wallpaper. I embraced all that, fell back on my own past, and resurrected it here in a more finished way. I knew the client would understand where it came from and like it."

OPPOSITE Framed hemisphere maps hanging from brass railings and a terra-cotta plaque of a befeathered Native American add historical interest to the stately staircase with its tall, arched window.

PRECEDING PAGES, LEFT Papered in a sprightly David Hicks wallpaper, the entrance hall has a warm, inviting ambience. At the hall's terminus, a bust of a Rhode Island Native American chieftain on a pedestal enhances a sense of place. **PRECEDING PAGES, RIGHT** Scheerer composed a casual, welcoming scene near the front door: an antler hat rack, a Gothic hall chair, and an umbrella stand that also holds errant golf clubs. **LEFT** The living room's mood is one of calm and lightness. A pale striped sofa and two-tone slipper chair give it a breezy nautical feeling that Scheerer reinforced by hanging watercolors of clipper ships and sailboats above the sofa; artist Mary Maguire adapted them from sailors' woolworks. The Chinese Chippendale coffee table tells a story about the nineteenth-century China trade that thrived in Colonial America.

ABOVE LEFT Scheerer filled the living room with vintage Bar Harbor wicker chairs to give it a summery feeling all year long, and he made liberal use of a distinctly American chintz. **TOP RIGHT** A Chinese screen, one of a pair, frames the view into another zone of the large living room. **ABOVE RIGHT** The arm of a nineteenth-century Swedish painted sofa has lyrical grace. **OPPOSITE** A large octagonal coffee table by Bielecky Brothers and a modern photograph of the ocean by Lynn Davis bring the room into the twenty-first century.

ABOVE AND RIGHT The dining room is Scheerer's Proustian madeleine—it is infused with the spirit of his grandmother's dining room in East Hampton (see page 6). Lyford Trellis wallpaper, its lattice the same color as the room's trim and moldings, creates the effect of an architectural framework. Clustered around a massive pedestal table, the dining chairs are upholstered in Provençal checks in back and a large-scale blue-and-white paisley pattern in front; the paisley print is Kashmir by Raoul Textiles, one of Scheerer's prized picks.

OPPOSITE Scheerer had the breakfast room table made to fit in this bay window. He discovered hand-painted Cuban tiles while doing work in the Bahamas; here he's chosen a bright blue medallion pattern. **ABOVE** In the family room, a games table set in a bay window is flanked by the scrolling profiles of bentwood chairs. Scheerer found a sheep sculpture inspired by François-Xavier Lalanne in the upstairs nursery and installed it here for fun and extra seating.

OPPOSITE The family room's plaster walls were enhanced with painted faux-bois paneling. The seat cushions on the blue sofa are slipcovered for easy cleaning and replacement when worn, a trick Scheerer uses for large or hard-living families. The chair is vintage wicker from Maine. The textured-wool lattice carpet is from Shyam Ahuja. **ABOVE, CLOCKWISE FROM TOP LEFT** The Indian-inspired orientalist paisley is by Peter Dunham; an authentic Portuguese woven-cotton ikat covers a wicker chair seat; wildflowers fill a blue-and-white pitcher; the sofa's contrasting seat cushions add informality.

Summer in Maine

After he bought his own house in Maine several years ago, Scheerer came to understand the Down East decorating idiom in a deep way. He knows summer in Maine is different from elsewhere. "It's fleeting and unpredictable," he says. "It's a place where a morning of fog rolling in is as beloved as an afternoon of sunshine. House interiors are important in ways they might not be at the beach."

In designing this house on Mount Desert Island for a family with entrenched summer roots in Maine, Scheerer looked back to the grand summer houses of nearby harbors. The Rockefellers, Fords, Astors, and several of the great lady decorators had rustic yet famously stylish houses around here. Sister Parish decorated Brooke Astor's house, and she had her own Maine "cottage" in nearby Dark Harbor.

"I may have been channeling Sister Parish," says Scheerer. "Although it was highly calculated, her look had a carefree spirit: lots of pattern, wicker, painted furniture, and flowery English chintzes. It's cozy, perfect for Maine, where the weather is bleaker than in other summer colonies." Scheerer's rendition of Sister Parish is decidedly sparer than the original, but it's equally attuned to comfort, and like hers, it's all about nostalgia and family life.

Scheerer had decorated for these clients before, and he recycled much of the furniture he'd selected for their previous country house, including the exuberant Belter-style Victorian sofa in the living room. The first time around he upholstered it, including most of the wooden frame, in a watery pink-and-yellow floral pattern printed on cotton mattress ticking. He figured he'd have to re-cover it this time so it would harmonize with new living room curtains in a classic multicolored chintz. But to his surprise, the two patterns got along. He realized he liked the unplanned effect of so many colors together, so instead of a tight color scheme, he was able to give the room a lively, improvisational soul. It's a slightly makeshift feeling, but in a lucky, cheerful, summer house way.

For the dining room, he concocted a chimerical mural by splicing together three Fitz Hugh Lane paintings from the 1890s—landscapes in which Lane, a nineteenth-century Luminist, depicts a pristine stretch of Somes Sound, the very same views from the room itself. The paintings have different scales and colorations so Scheerer had them digitized, then manipulated into a continuous, sepia-toned scene that spans all four walls and approximates the feeling of a hand-painted mural.

Upstairs, in a bedroom for two girls, he took a potentially old-hat fern print that's been festooning country clubs for decades and made it modern by using it to upholster a long, midcentury-inspired headboard that ties two beds together. The print nicely illustrates the *genius loci* as well. "Maine is a wonderland of ferns," Scheerer says. "One of the principal activities there is walking around the woods, trying not to step on them."

But there are fusty elements in this house that he didn't even try to rejuvenate. In the guest room, twin beds with chenille candlewick bedspreads are proudly dowdy—so confidently unadorned that they present themselves as radiantly fresh. It's an instance of Scheerer's magical ability to embrace the passé or the provincial and mysteriously make them chic. He's always been a big proponent of twin beds, and if there is a resurgence of them these days, he is partly responsible.

Twin beds are "old-fashioned, circumspect, and kind of nice," he once said in a *House Beautiful* interview. "There's nothing worse than a thirteen-year-old child in a queen-sized bed. It's just too awful. And I don't know any couple over the age of forty-five who could care less—they look forward to sleeping in twin beds. I have had people fighting over my twin guest room."

OPPOSITE With all the bedrooms radiating from it, the upstairs hallway is the core of the house. The rustic Black Forest mirror is a cartoon-like surprise at the top of the stairs. Scheerer painted the original dark paneling and stairs white. In the background, bird prints lead the way to a guest room.

OPPOSITE Scheerer used faux-bois wallpaper to add interest to the entrance hall. Hung on the front door, a harness of sleigh bells signals arrival. The English spoolwork bench is covered with patterned pillows and surrounded by primitive bird prints. Coarse woven coir matting from Beauvais Carpets covers the floor. **ABOVE** A bust of Benjamin Franklin watches over the entrance. Franklin founded the University of Pennsyvania, America's first university, from which both owners graduated.

ABOVE Scheerer arranged bird prints up and down a staircase. The stairs are dressed up with a runner of striped sisal and cotton. The intriguing L-shaped step basket is an old American labor-saving convenience. **OPPOSITE** The large Noguchi lantern made of rice paper and bamboo plays off the shape of the arched window. It fills up and gives scale to the space. **OVERLEAF** With its spirited mix of furnishings, the living room is Scheerer's Sister-Parish-in-Maine moment. A Saarinen modernist coffee table, a new Moroccan rug, vintage Bar Harbor wicker wing chairs, and classic chintz curtains combine to make a winning statement that's also pure Scheerer. Found in a church thrift shop, the undulating Victorian sofa became modern and sculptural when Scheerer covered it in a fresh print.

OPPOSITE The other end of the living room features an antique Windsor rocker, chosen because it adds life without blocking the view. "It's anthropomorphic," says Scheerer, attuned to the souls of antiques. "It's like having Ichabod Crane in the room." **TOP, FROM LEFT TO RIGHT** A backgammon set on a vintage card table; a framed oval of decoupaged bird egg images by Sheila Potter; an antique iron basketball hoop standing on its own bracket. **ABOVE** Scheerer designed the Syrie Maugham–style sofa and upholstered it in orange mattress ticking.

ABOVE Scheerer transformed landscape paintings by Fitz Hugh Lane into a lush sepia-toned mural that wraps around the dining room. A Chinese demilune console is topped with a Nantucket lightship basket mirror. **OPPOSITE** Bentwood chairs surround a painted wood table of Scheerer's design.

LEFT Boldly scaled Adam's Eden wallpaper by Carleton V transforms the guest bedroom into a delightful arbor. The candlewick bedspreads are a Scheerer signature. **ABOVE** Gauzy bed hangings and a clear glass bottle lamp add ethereal charm.

ABOVE To let a bit of the original house shine through, Scheerer left existing pine paneling in a bedroom for two sisters. The position of the doors dictated the size and shape of the long headboard upholstered in Botanical Fern by Schumacher. **RIGHT** In a room for a young boy who proudly sleeps in a bed that belonged to his grandfather, Scheerer used Spatter wallpaper by Hinson, one of his favorites. A State of Maine flag bought on the Internet is swagged between bedposts.

OPPOSITE Scheerer suggested the addition of this spacious porch overlooking Somes Sound. He furnished one side of it in a mix of all-weather wicker, teak, and terra-cotta furniture. **TOP LEFT** The back door of the house has a forthright Maine look. **ABOVE LEFT** A beautiful monogrammed plate is complemented by up-to-date tabletop accessories. **ABOVE RIGHT** The other side of the porch is set up for outdoor dining with a picnic-style table and benches upholstered in weatherproof fabric.

TO HIS ADMIRERS, ONE OF THE MOST APPEALing and distinctive features of Tom Scheerer's work is that he prefers to underdecorate. He often finds himself in the curious position of trying to get clients to be comfortable with less renovating, fewer objects, and less embellishment. In fact, Scheerer's low-key, improvisational decorating style is in some ways a reaction to—and an implicit critique of— the overblown, grandiose houses of our age.

"It's my general philosophy to accept what's given and make it work without going to too much trouble," he says. "It's what makes one house different from the next. Why rip out a bathroom to spend $20,000 on designer tile just to have a bathroom that looks exactly like everyone else's? Why not bleach the sink, put a new scalloped lampshade on the sconce, and get on with life? That's what we did in our summer houses in the old days—it's why they had charm."

With this Colonial-era house in the historic village of Sag Harbor, New York, Scheerer had additional reason for leaving the project a touch underbaked. His young clients are avid players in the sport of antiquing. "They really enjoy the process of meeting me at an antiques fair, paying cash for a painting, and having me whack it onto the wall five minutes later," Scheerer says. The couple has a lifetime of collecting ahead, and Scheerer wanted to leave room for their finds.

The combination office and sitting room that Scheerer made for the husband is pristine, spare, and all but free of ornament. Many clients would not be comfortable with this degree of airy, arty minimalism, but this couple appears to be game for forays into modernism. "To me it has the look of a country doctor's office," Scheerer says. "The wonderfully animated Danish stove reinforces the feeling."

The Zen atmosphere of the master bedroom came with the house. Meticulously handcrafted in cedar by Japanese artisans commissioned by the previous owner, it is serene and almost spa-like. The clients might not have undertaken such an exotic installation themselves, but they are glad to be the beneficiaries. "It's like a trip to a Kyoto ryokan without having to sleep on the floor," Scheerer says. He made suitable accents to the architecture. The headboard is covered in a modern fabric reminiscent of antique Japanese indigo prints. A Noguchi paper lantern, a translucent white sphere, is echoed by the round dressing mirror suspended like the moon in front of a window.

A Clean Canvas

The dining room's midnight blue walls were conceived as a background for—and a sponge to soak up—the spoils of weekend buying adventures. Its wild-mushroom cap of a hanging light fixture is by Ingo Maurer, made from paper fans in the 1970s. "I have a special thing for vintage Maurer fixtures," says Scheerer, whose thriftiness goes right out the window when it comes to certain modernist artists. Scheerer arranged pots of succulents and hurricanes on the lustrous tabletop. The dining room is a passageway through the house, so the table needs to look dressed even when it's not being used.

Scheerer found some fine antiques to ground the house in Sag Harbor's storied past as a whaling village. The dining room's Irish console with a bow front is sublime in its simplicity. In the breakfast room, the combback Windsor chairs bristle with life. "They feel sea captainy without being literal," he says.

As in the houses Scheerer makes for himself, this one contains found objects displayed to add wonder and serendipity to the mood. In the living room, he let a painted wooden seagull alight on the coffee table and steal the show. "Found it at one of those summer antiques fairs," he says of the bird, whose wings are outspread for landing. "I got there early, walked around with it proudly, and had people trailing behind me in envy."

OPPOSITE In the monastic study, Scheerer removed a fancy brick fireplace and replaced it with a chaste Shaker-inspired wood stove by Wittus. Its assymetrical design makes the room feel more dynamic. The scrolling arms of an American Empire chair add contrasting curves.

OPPOSITE The Japanese-style master bedroom came with the house and Scheerer decorated it appropriately. The headboard is covered in a fabric reminiscent of Japanese indigo prints. Bedside lamps are made from woven Japanese headrests. Bedside tables are by Frank Lloyd Wright. **ABOVE** Shoji screens shield his and hers dressing areas. A mirror hangs over a dressing table like the moon, echoing the shape of a Noguchi rice paper lantern. The 1950s AP-27 armchair by Hans Wegner is a fittingly spare adornment.

ABOVE For a guest bathroom, Scheerer designed pink-and-white gingham wallpaper that recalls a room in his family's East Hampton beach house down the road. A glass-fronted apothecary cabinet serves as a linen closet. **OPPOSITE** A carved owl stands guard over a boy's bedroom. Simple iron beds are laid with pick-stitch quilts. The astronomy prints were found at a summer antiques fair.

ABOVE The heart of this house is the dining room, where midnight blue walls make a graphic backdrop for the owner's burgeoning collection of weekend finds. Under the Long Island map is a mixed-media collage by Scheerer. The bark overcoat is a thrift-store find that was probably made as a liquor bottle display; the swoopy, biomorphic, Art Nouveau brass and wood swan's-neck lamp is from Scott Estepp Gallery. **RIGHT** The lacquered dining table is the color of vanilla ice cream. Featherweight but sturdy Japanese rattan chairs are from Yamakawa. Ingo Maurer's 1970s pendant is made out of Japanese fans.

OPPOSITE In the kitchen, Scheerer replaced some of the lower cabinetry with a window-seat banquette. The owner had seen too many Saarinen tables and didn't want one as a breakfast table, so Scheerer compromised, designing a Saarinen-shaped top on a more traditional base. The Windsor captain's chairs are midcentury. ABOVE A nineteenth-century Spanish Colonial glass-fronted cabinet displays china and bibelots. The extra captain's chair can be moved to the breakfast room as needed.

A CLEAN CANVAS . 125

BELOW A long living room with a modernist vibe was fashioned from the original double parlor. The yellow painting is by East Hampton artist Tony Stubbing. "It has a Jackson Pollock in Springs feeling," says Scheerer. The eccentric wooden wing chair references its upholstered forebears. **OPPOSITE TOP, FROM LEFT TO RIGHT** A Brancusi wooden side table sporting a Japanese bowl; a dynamic, summery painted seagull; a Japanese blue-and-white plate. **OPPOSITE BOTTOM** Café curtains maximize the light while providing privacy. Blue Baldwin-style St. Thomas sofas add deep comfort.

A CLEAN CANVAS . 127

Tropics

Conjuring Old Florida

In a civilized old Florida enclave perfumed by orange trees, the houses come mostly in two styles: Spanish Colonial and Florida Regency, many by the masters Marion Sims Wyeth, John Volk, and Maurice Fatio. Having grown up in and among these houses, the client was fond of the genres but wary of the grandeur. She was considering building a new house for herself, and after she was introduced to Scheerer, it became clear that both were casting about for something a bit different.

But what? Early in the process, a daughter-in-law appeared with a snapshot of a modest coral stone building she'd recently seen in the Florida Keys. Eureka! They'd found the solution to the simplicity they were seeking in the elemental building material. "We decided to avoid historicism and go for this vernacular style," says Scheerer. "The coral stone has a resonance in the history of old Florida. We knew its beautiful rough and varied texture would provide a wonderful substantiality and patina."

During a three-year collaboration with the client and the architect, Tom Kirchhoff, several unconventional ideas emerged about how this coral stone house would be lived in. "There are deliberate episodes of quirky informality balanced by gestures of grand scale in the house," Scheerer says. "The main entry moment happens in the open air." The moment, as Scheerer calls it, is a lofty stone-clad pavilion, its doorway framed by tall, curving shutters. He furnished it with a carved-teak table base he had made in India to support a Moroccan tile top he found on the Dixie Highway in West Palm Beach. An ancient silvery banyan tree on the property was moved to the parking court just outside the pavilion. In a stroke of genius, the landscape designer, Cecilia De Grelle, placed it slightly off of the main axis. Imperfectly framed by the open doorway, this leviathan of a tree twists up, shading the graveled precinct like the soul of grace and magnificence.

As elaborate and extensive as this house is, its rooms feel surprisingly relaxed. The peacock blue dining room is as down to earth as it is exotic. Chairs of beachy bleached oak and caning were adapted from a chair Scheerer had noticed in a Manhattan ladies' club. The kitchen's eccentric vintage Ingo Maurer light fixture made of paper fans floats breezily over the island, and the ebullient breakfast room has, among other assets, an oval Saarinen tulip table with a sensuous driftwood-like top crafted for the client.

The principal guest room is, to Scheerer's mind, one of the finest he has done. A quintessential old-fashioned bedroom of opulent scale, its debts are all to the great midcentury American decorators: Ruby Ross Wood, Eleanor McMillen Brown, and Billy Baldwin. "It was loosely inspired by a wonderful black-and-white photo in *Billy Baldwin Remembers*— a Palm Beach bedroom even then long gone," Scheerer says. Freshness, gaiety, and innocence converge. Thanks to a remarkable chintz rescued from oblivion, a confetti of airy blossoms blankets everything from the walls to the blithe dresser; Scheerer had the discontinued print recolored and reproduced from a treasured fabric document. "It's one of those classic American prints, so nostalgic for me and happily, too, for the client," Scheerer says.

The four-poster bed was crafted in India and at ten feet tall it presides over the room. The windows are curtained and topped with tailored pennant valances. The wing chair's skirt has a scalloped edge, another light-hearted Scheerer touch. "It's a way of giving a shapely wing chair a little further charm," he says.

Such old-fashioned decorating done with crispness and clarity will probably figure prominently in Scheerer's future. In the library, the classic Bridgewater sofa is covered in a familiar French print, La Rivière Enchantée. "It's an old saw," Scheerer says, recolored here in a vivid azure for the tropics. The lamps are traditional, fashioned from Chinese storage jars, yet bold in scale and emphatic in tonality. The room has been given a voluptuous coziness that comes from excellent upholstery and good-quality antiques. Yet it wears its finery with a breezy touch.

OPPOSITE This house is built of indigenous Florida coral stone, which has more texture and variation than Dominican coquina, the variety used most often in Florida. An enfilade of indoor/outdoor spaces leads to the front door proper. Hanging over the entrance loggia is a lantern Scheerer designed for the Urban Electric Company.

ABOVE In the entrance pavilion, the teak table base and matching mirror were designed by Scheerer to mimic the fish-scale Moroccan tile tabletop. He also designed the clamshell sconces in cast resin, being careful not to make the shells identical. OPPOSITE A terra-cotta pelican adds caprice to the view of the old banyan tree shading the parking court. The triangular lantern's faux candle glows just like the real thing.

PRECEDING PAGES A rough-textured pecky cypress ceiling was paired with the house's coral stone walls in the loggia, conceived as the main living room. Concealed shutters can be rolled down in inclement weather. Antique Morris chairs with adjustable backs, classic American wicker chairs from Bielecky Brothers, and Japanese rattan chairs are linked by color and texture. They make a casual and decidedly undressy mix. **OPPOSITE** In the mud room, an Indo-Portuguese inlaid dressing table and tin repoussé mirror are both functional and atmospheric. **ABOVE LEFT** Known for his mythically familiar Americana scenes, artist Kevin Paulsen painted a charming tropical version with local flora and fauna on the walls of the ladies' powder room. **ABOVE RIGHT** The men's dressing room is outfitted with an exuberant Regency dressing table refitted as a sink with a marble top. On the walls is a collection of nineteenth-century palm-leaf prints by J. Barbosa Rodrigues, a Brazilian botanist.

BELOW The tiered Ingo Maurer vintage light fixture adds an artful touch and personality to an otherwise serene kitchen. Cabinets are made from pecky cypress for a driftwood feeling. Beyond the kitchen, the walls of the butler's pantry are clad in Cuban tiles.
OPPOSITE The owner found the standard white laminate top of the Saarinen tables Scheerer favors too cold, so he made one with a custom cerused-oak top for the sun-flooded breakfast room. The undulant camelback sofa was made to order. Lamps were fashioned from antique pickle jars, an old-fashioned Americana touch in tropical aqua.

ABOVE LEFT Vibrant English transferware plates depict oranges and orange blossoms. The owner doesn't fear snakes and collects them in all forms. A jointed garter snake adorns the table and a grouping of nineteenth-century French watercolors of snakes hangs in the nearby pantry. **TOP AND ABOVE RIGHT** Painted wooden parrots perch on the dining table among cuttings of a feathery topical vine. **OPPOSITE** For an elaborate house, the dining room has a strikingly casual feeling. Its balconied doors overlook a courtyard, so its peacock blue walls always frame riotous tropical greenery. Scheerer made the round painted-wood table and designed the rattan and bleached-oak dining chairs, an adaptation of a chair he glimpsed at the Colony Club in Manhattan. The fan wall sconces by Ingo Maurer are vintage.

For a supremely old-fashioned guest bedroom that's restrained and completely correct yet exuberant, Scheerer had a long-held-on-to piece of a discontinued document chintz copied so he could envelop the room in it. The dresser was painted to match by Brian Leaver. The tall Anglo-Indian-style bed of ebonized teak was made in India.

OPPOSITE A vintage rattan chaise covered in pale pink linen with cotton brush fringe adds a 1930s vibe. The Venetian-style etched-glass mirror is an extremely proper accoutrement for a proper room. **ABOVE** Above a bathtub set in a chaste niche clad in horizontal cypress paneling, a French pocket-watch mirror made of rope dangles jauntily. The ubiquitous bell-jar lantern, used in the right place in a deep color—peacock blue—shows how Scheerer can make momentous design out of ordinary elements.

Oriented away from the water view for coziness, the sumptuous library faces a leafy courtyard. Scheerer used a classic English-style fringed sofa. He found the fine nineteenth-century Anglo-Indian caned chair, right, at Cove Landing. Antique Chinese storage jars were made into the substantial lamps flanking the sofa.

OPPOSITE A Milton Avery painting was reframed in light driftwood to contrast with the library's pecky cypress walls. The lions' mask sconces came from Paris. Two upholstered Ward Bennett tub chairs can swivel away from the fireplace to face other seating groups. ABOVE Scheerer designed a pair of black lacquer and wicker slipper chairs, adapting them from a Jean-Michel Frank design. OVERLEAF, LEFT A casual upstairs sitting room off the master bedroom has grasscloth walls stenciled in a Mughal-inspired pattern. Scheerer has always been fond of wicker peacock chairs and threw this one into the mix with its matching footstool just for fun. "We call this room the snoratorium—it's where somebody can go when they're sick or the other one's snoring," Scheerer says. The daybed sofa can also serve as a napping spot. OVERLEAF, RIGHT In a ground-floor study, dark brown walls contrast with the lavender, purple, and ultramarine color scheme. The carpet is a vintage cotton and jute dhurrie, purchased after the room was designed—a lucky find. The desk was made in India.

Palm Beach Pied-à-Terre

Decorating in the tropics comes in a nuanced range of tones. Palm Beach style has an urbanity as well as a grandly exotic aspect that makes it decidedly different from, say, the informal, beachy feel of the Bahamas.

Scheerer warms to tropical décor in all its permutations and he likes keeping intricate tonal distinctions. Focusing on the crisp and citified side of tropical style, he took a three-bedroom, low-rise apartment with low ceilings and turned it into a civilized gathering spot for a Manhattan book publisher, his wife, and their children.

The apartment's front door opens on an irregularly shaped space that serves as its entry, living, and dining areas. To create a sense of discrete rooms and to make a more ceremonious arrival spot, Scheerer dreamed up the notion of the large cylindrical book tower, which also handily plays into a bookish theme in keeping with the owner's profession.

"We made it to fit in segments," he says of the prodigious teakwood tower. "And stacked them like poker chips." Arranged with books and objects, it screens an immediate view of the living room and Lake Worth beyond. Like a protruding boulder in a river, it also directs the flow, creating natural routes to the bedroom hall, the living room, and the kitchen.

The Lake Worth panorama became a sultry backdrop for the dining area. Scheerer furnished it with a Saarinen tulip table and Italian wicker dining chairs that take the chill off the hard-edged, high-risey feeling. The living room's superb cobra-like lounge chairs are from the same manufacturer, Vittorio Bonacina, one of Scheerer's hallowed sources for great contemporary design.

Defined by mirror, Formica, wicker, and potted palms, the living room is a distillate of vintage modern cool. With its white laminate coffee table, pair of sky blue sofas, and those boldly undulant Italian wicker chairs, this room is definitely on vacation. Palm fronds swoon over the sofa and hurricanes flicker with candles at the cocktail hour.

Scheerer gave each bedroom its own transporting atmosphere. The master has a fanciful Venetian-style upholstered bed in a combination of tropical grasscloth and cotton ikat. The platform, with its handsomely shaped legs, was designed by Scheerer, who is not so fond of bed skirts. The radiant girls' room features one of his favorite flower prints, Spring Garden, by Raoul Textiles. "I never tire of it," Scheerer says. "It's all the things I like in a print: fresh, cheerful, graphic…lots of air." Like a men's haberdashery or a safari camp, the boys' room is outfitted with midcentury lamps, dresser, and Edward Wormley Janus chairs that recall Palm Beach's midcentury glamour. Chinese watercolors of tigers lend an exotic, adventurous vibe.

"It's sparer and crisper than the way this family lives in New York," Scheerer says of the apartment. "Its arrangements are deliberate set pieces. It's a true pied-à-terre, a place without too many personal objects to encumber them or stifle the languor. They come and go easily. They can get down from New York before lunch!"

OPPOSITE The brass and teak secretary was made to take advantage of every available inch of the room's height. A Serge Roche–style standing lamp offers a bold contrast to delphinium blue grasscloth walls.

LEFT The foyer's substantial circular book tower was custom made in India. The bentwood settee offers an airy, buoyant contrast. **ABOVE LEFT** Chinese lanterns float over the living room in a painting by Donald Sultan. **ABOVE RIGHT** A two-tiered Formica coffee table designed by Scheerer displays a set of wooden books. **BELOW** A new Saarinen dining table surrounded by Vittorio Bonacina wicker chairs overlooks the Lake Worth waterfront.

PRECEDING PAGES A pair of Baldwin-style St. Thomas sofas provide deep comfort in the living room, where a mirrored wall reflects the view. The sinuous wicker chairs by Vittorio Bonacina lend a sculptural elegance. **LEFT** A girls' bedroom with sheetrock walls was fortified with Nobilis faux-bois wallpaper arranged in horizontal panels. Installed without a visible rod, the diaphanous curtains give the room an illusion of height. Mirrored panels behind the valanced bed hangings increase the sense of space. **ABOVE** Raoul Textile's Secret Garden cotton print is repeated on the drawer face of the dresser. Tole palm tree lamps are a staple of Palm Beach style. **OVERLEAF, LEFT** In the master bedroom, a spirited Venetian-style bed combines woven ikat and grasscloth. Lacquered blue wallpaper adds shimmer. **OVERLEAF, RIGHT** With walls upholstered in a striped fabric reminiscent of a military tent, the boy's bedroom has an exotic campaign air. The Janus chair, a vintage classic, is by Edward Wormley, and the 1960s Danish lamps are from the Holmegaard Glassworks.

BORN WITH A RESTLESS NATURE, SCHEERER is an enthusiastic and inveterate traveler. If an opportunity arises to visit a city he hasn't been to yet, he needs no convincing to step onto an airplane. Recent trips to Burma, Mexico, Cuba, Morocco, and India have given him inspiration and new visual territory.

Part of his pleasure is in stockpiling smart, offbeat imagery to sprinkle throughout his decorating projects. He understands how a regional aesthetic, its architectural forms, and even its practical details can seem like otherworldly glamour back home.

In this case, the client had grown up in her parents' Spanish Revival house in Hobe Sound, Florida. Many years later, she and her husband bought the land next door, doubling their lot size, and began to think about building their own more expansive house in the same style. They hired Merrill, Pastor & Colgan Architects, a firm renowned for its work in the tropics, particularly at Windsor, Florida, fifty miles up the road. Scheerer joined the Hobe Sound project soon thereafter and was instrumental in tweaking the intricacies of the plan and in choosing finishes for textural richness.

"We avoided the obvious conventions when shopping for tiles," he remembers. "The loggia tiles are not Spanish or Moroccan but midcentury Italian. We were told the same tiles are found in il Papa's bedroom! That was enough for us!"

Scheerer fashioned the tall, airy living room to serve almost as a club room for the cocktail parties, buffets, and bridge games that are customary concomitants to life in Hobe Sound. "The slightly exotic atmosphere tends to get parties off the ground," he says.

Spurred by memories of Shangri-La, Doris Duke's grand Mughal-inspired estate in Honolulu, he designed two deeply tufted banquettes upholstered in an orientalist paisley (alas, an extinct one) to make use of the corners. Just as enchantingly festive and fanciful are the white wooden *jalis* (traceried screens) he designed to cover the largest bank of windows. On the other side of the room he devised a more gently transporting seating group around a fireplace. A printed shawl Scheerer carried from India as a gift to the client found its way to warm up the sofa. On the walls, he used his trompe l'oeil bark paper device, applying it in squares to mimic stone blocks. Part of what amuses him about the manuever is how mere paper adds such impressive heft to a soaring expanse of wall.

Knowing curtains would have spoiled the purity of the dining room's arched windows, Scheerer left them bare and brought comfort to the room with upholstered saber-back dining chairs. Whitewashed pecky cypress and antiqued mirror panels lend 1930s-style dash.

The table is the confluence of luck and ingenuity—a gift from the cosmos that Scheerer knew what to do with. Midstream in planning this room, he found out that the carved dolphin base was coming up for auction from the estate of Doris Duke and he snapped it up. In Duke's day the base had a glass top, but Scheerer avoids cold surfaces for tables. He had it fitted with an elbow-friendly, rustic wood top.

The graceful swan tureen used as a centerpiece has a particular resonance. "One of the charms of this house is that it overlooks miles of golf course and estuary," Scheerer says. "The bird life is amazing. The wife spends hours puttering out of doors, making sure the herons, egrets, pelicans, and cygnets are doing okay."

At night, when all the birds are safely tucked in, the house lights up like a lantern. A long pool shimmers in a courtyard. "It's like the *Arabian Nights*, but not taken too far," Scheerer says.

Glamour and Exotica

OPPOSITE A peristyle courtyard by Merrill, Pastor & Colgan Architects forms an entry sequence and connects the two wings of the house. Scheerer was instrumental in selecting the house's rich and varied array of materials, including pecky cypress, recycled terra-cotta tiles, and coquina stone.

A vast living room with eighteen-foot-high ceilings has the luxury of multiple seating areas. The large chandelier humanizes the space and helps fill up its soaring volume. Italian candle screens on the far wall conceal electric lighting. Not long after it was unveiled, this room became the talk of the town with its combination of French furnishings and exotic elements. In high season, it's the scene of convivial cocktail gatherings, buffets, and bridge parties.

ABOVE, CLOCKWISE FROM TOP LEFT Details of the living room that add an exotic layer: a box with bone inlay, a traditional Indian craft; a custom card table designed by Scheerer; another bone-inlaid box; an intricately carved and inlaid coffee table. **OPPOSITE** The orientalist fabric on tufted, L-shaped banquettes generated the color scheme and set the tone of the room.

ABOVE In a powder room off the library, a French faux-bamboo dressing table was converted into a washstand. Lyford Trellis wallpaper in brown and cream enhances the architecture with its vintage-style fretwork. **OPPOSITE** Scheerer used pecky cypress again for the library's walls. Made-to-order Cole Porter bookcases add sparkle and provide a contrast to the rough-hewn walls. Grasscloth window shades filter strong light. The shepherd's crook armchair facing the window is covered in white ostrich.

PRECEDING PAGES, LEFT The dining room walls are paneled in whitewashed pecky cypress alternating with antiqued mirror. The carved dolphin table base from the estate of Doris Duke has a round wooden top. Saber-back dining chairs are upholstered in a celery green Fortuny-esque printed cotton. **PRECEDING PAGES, TOP RIGHT** Under the gaze of a swan, the table is set for lunch. **PRECEDING PAGES, BOTTOM RIGHT** A potted tole aloe atop a pecky cypress column provides permanent greenery. **ABOVE LEFT** Three-quarter-sized beds with tailored bed hangings add an extra level of comfort to a feminine guest room. Daylight enlivens a purple glass bottle lamp. **ABOVE RIGHT** The pair of paintings above the chair are by Sally Michel, the widow of Milton Avery. **OPPOSITE** Raoul Textile's Secret Garden fabric wallcovering transforms another guest room into a nostalgic bower. The wicker beds are from the owner's girlhood.

OPPOSITE Italian glazed-ceramic tiles pave the floor of the rear loggia, an outdoor living room furnished mostly in 1930s-style rattan pieces designed by Scheerer. On the far wall, a deep banquette invites lounging. **ABOVE** The master bedroom's balcony overlooks the loggia and swimming pool. The three elements together make for a glamorous scene day and night.

The Simple Life

WHEN TOM SCHEERER FIRST SET FOOT on Harbour Island, Bahamas, a tiny island off Eleuthera, the renowned paradise with a colonial past and pink sand beaches was experiencing a turnover from an old guard of New Englanders and Midwesterners who had quietly maintained it for decades to a younger, more international set. India Hicks, the Miller sisters, Ron Perlman, and Mickey Drexler, among others, were shaking things up.

This jazzy crowd sparked a boom of fancier, more elaborate tropical houses than the island had seen to date. It was in this ramped-up climate that Scheerer was asked to build and decorate several houses. Never one to waste a good opportunity, he acquired a large fixer-upper for himself and then a second, much smaller one a few years later. While others were going in the opposite direction, Harbour Island turned out to be a perfect place for him to fulfill his long-held fantasy of living with radical simplicity in the tropics.

Scheerer credits his friend Elsa Peretti, the Italian modernist jewelry designer and tastemaker, for opening his eyes. "In some ways, she lives like a peasant," he says of Peretti. "That's her goal. She has as much appreciation for a brown bentwood chair or a heart-shaped rock found on the beach as she does for a Holbein miniature portrait. Of course, she's got houses all over, but she's probably sleeping in a single bed right now, in a rustic room with the window open."

Scheerer's saltbox was built in 1800, an English loyalist cottage made from coral stone blocks quarried from its own basement. It sits across the street from what used to be his larger, more elaborate house, a former convent from the same era. The smaller one was in a state of ruin and utterly ruled out for consideration by the island's new guard. But when a hotelier began making plans to turn it into a late-night piano bar, Scheerer snapped it up to keep his neighborhood quiet. The house had rudimentary plumbing, disintegrating floorboards, a rotting roof, and a gang of resident cats, none of which fazed him. His thought was to transform it into a guest house annex. He renovated it lightly and furnished it simply, mostly from catalogues and vintage shops, nevertheless endowing it with tremendous romance and charm. "It's not particularly Bahamian," he says. "It's actually my reverie of Greek island life."

Everything is kept deliberately low-tech. There's a washing machine but no dryer, so he hangs laundry on a clothesline. He usually forsakes the bathroom for the outdoor shower. Only two downstairs bedrooms have glass in the windows and air conditioning to stave off the heat of Bahamian summer nights. The remaining windows have neither panes nor screens. "We use a lot of bug spray!" he says cheerfully.

Scheerer is a resourceful, inventive cook who uses the limited local produce to turn out simple, Italian-inspired dishes. In his hands, entertaining is an easy art form. Here, without fuss, he sets a chic table with whatever he finds in the garden and the cupboard and puts on lunch and dinner at the drop of a straw hat. In his primitive kitchen, he used hand-poured Cuban cement tiles for flooring and installed a 1930s four-burner enamel stove. "It looked right—and I didn't want to break the spell of the room." But he prefers to cook in the fireplace, his stand-in for an outdoor grill. There's not much counter space and no dishwasher, but he never minds snapping beans outside or doing dishes by hand and letting them dry on the wood rack above the cast-iron farm sink.

"It's a point of pride for me to show people that it makes sense to live this way, especially in a place where it's tough to do things the way we do them in New York," he says. "The truth is, I really don't need a SubZero refrigerator, a dishwasher, and a Viking range. In the decorating world, these are practically the givens these days. But fancy, sophisticated people who have borrowed or rented this house have come away amazed by it. They realize they don't need all the stuff that they thought was de rigueur."

OPPOSITE In an attic bedroom, an iron campaign bed from Anthropologie capitalizes on every inch of ceiling height. Laid with a sturdy, classic matelassé bedcover, the bed floats mid-room. Conical reading lights hung from the ceiling keep Scheerer from tripping over lamp cords. Walls are painted seafoam green, a nod to a Harbour Island old wives' tale about the wasp-repellant properties of the color green.

ABOVE In a downstairs bathroom, the pickled-teak washstand was made in India. The mirror, its frame painted with military motifs, hung in Scheerer's childhood nursery, a gift from his grandmother. **OPPOSITE** The cheerful entry hall shows Scheerer's work at its best and simplest: straw hats and bags hanging nonchalantly on the wall, a clear bottle lamp atop a junk-shop table with cabriole legs painted white, and baskets of beach necessities tucked below.

ABOVE Scheerer added an upstairs bathroom at the rear of the attic and painted it seafoam green. To keep the vernacular feeling of the room, he went to a lot of trouble to import an ordinary vintage cast-iron claw-foot tub from the United States. The windows above it are neither glazed nor screened. OPPOSITE Under the eaves in the attic bedroom, a beat-up 1950s dresser entirely without pedigree holds gingham shirts, white pants, and swimsuits. The coral lamp came from Pier One. Seashells in Plexiglas boxes were a gift from a client.

ABOVE AND RIGHT Initially an outbuilding, the kitchen was being used as a storage hut when Scheerer bought the property. He connected it to the main house and restored it lightly. Its fireplace was hidden behind a wall of pink-painted plywood, which he promptly removed so he could start cooking. To sustain the primitive mood, Scheerer imported a farm sink from the United States. He installed Cuban tile floors similar to those found in many old Harbour Island village houses. A fine American pine drop-leaf table is surrounded by antique bentwood chairs. One of the photographs hanging above the table is a well-known portrait of Picasso in his own kitchen by Robert Doisneau.

The kitchen opens onto a covered porch with louvered shutters and an open-air dining area. **OPPOSITE** Woven-fiberglass chairs circle a teak table shaded by a fringed Indonesian umbrella. **TOP LEFT** The table is set for a casual lunch with faux-bois china and striped placemats. **TOP RIGHT** A bentwood rocker with a plump striped pillow makes a comfortable reading perch. **ABOVE** Scheerer uses a few of his signature weathered-teak nesting cubes as modern side tables. The outdoor shower and laundry shed are out of sight behind the bamboo fencing.

Natural Selections

IN ARCHITECTURE AND DECORATING, MATERIALS are charged with meaning and mood. Scheerer almost always gravitates to the least slick version of a material and tries to use those that most aptly express the spirit of a place.

His favorite woods look wind scoured and wave tossed, especially the ones he uses in the tropics. The tiles he likes are irregular or hand painted. When choosing fabric, he avoids anything flashy or over-engineered. Even the contrarian's stamp of approval he bestows on white Formica for dining and cocktail tabletops is telling—he likes it because it seems unreconstructed, almost generic. In his Manhattan office recently, while searching through a huge inventory of sculptural, high-end ceiling fans online, he asked, "Don't they have anything normal and brown?"

When a couple with five children hired him to renovate, decorate, and landscape a compound of 1950s houses they'd just bought on Harbour Island in the Bahamas, Scheerer rearranged the functions of the various buildings and created furnished courtyards between them. Then he fashioned rooms with a lyrical naturalness, rich in textures as well as soft, matte surfaces netted with light and shadow.

The clients have strong roots in South Africa, which inspired some of Scheerer's ideas. Both South Africa and Curaçao, the Dutch Colonial island outpost, are known for the Cape Dutch style of architecture, characterized by distinctive bell-shaped gable ends. Scheerer appropriated the bell shape, using it as a fanciful top for a garden gate. In a guest room, he used the shape again as a quirky fireplace surround with an infill of blue and white *pique assiette*, or broken crockery mosaic. "The shard mosaic is a natural thing to do on Harbour Island," Scheerer says.

"Every yard in the village is an archaeological site with astounding amounts of discarded broken pottery. We think it's left over from the British loyalist era."

The library can be opened to the elements via large French-style casements, so the materials used in the room needed to be rustic. "On Harbour Island there are lots of maintenance issues, so you want things that will patina as nicely as possible," Scheerer says. He lined its walls in pecky cypress rubbed with lime to evoke driftwood. Glinting green bottle lamps invite the outdoors in. Scheerer had the large bookcase, two end tables, a coffee table, and twin pineapple beds in a girls' bedroom fabricated in India out of pickled teak. Its pale, unvarnished surface has a relaxed, tactile grace, and it's a natural on Harbour Island because it's weather and bug resistant.

In accordance with local tradition, most houses on Harbour Island have a name. Scheerer renamed this one The Beehive because the owners' surname begins with a B and, with so many children running around, it's a hive of activity. He found a vintage painted shop sign depicting a bee skep and hung it in their dining room. "We made a few other corny moves. For the amusement of the children, I had bees embroidered on the slipcovers," he says. Dining chairs with straw backs and seats add strong texture, and the commodious Brazilian trestle table has its own plainspoken patina.

Throughout the house, there's a dialogue between earthy elements and the old-fashioned Harbour Island preppy factor. Nothing seems contrived or out of place. The vocabulary of materials and furniture styles is all Scheerer's, yet somehow it looks like it could have been stylistic happenstance—but only in a perfect world. "It's for people who want to live comfortably and smartly, but not glitzily," Scheerer says.

OPPOSITE A fireplace surround in a guest bedroom makes a graphic statement. It's an example of the domestic craft known as *pique assiette*, or broken crockery mosaic. Scheerer designed the painted wooden framework, which he had carved in India, to mimic the gable ends of traditional Cape Dutch architecture.

OPPOSITE By adding the Cape Dutch gable motif as an elegant fillip to the top of the formerly plain gateway to the compound, Scheerer set a lively South African tone without tearing anything down.
TOP The addition of an outdoor sitting area to a storage building created a relaxed waterside boathouse.
ABOVE Scheerer connected the buildings in the compound with pathways and verandas. This covered passageway shelters the doors to the children's bedrooms.

On the main veranda, Scheerer restored the traditional painted-wood lounge furniture that came with the house and fitted it with practical brown strié Sunbrella cushions. The large, low, stone-topped teak table was a Scheerer addition. Beyond this outdoor living room is the guest house with its own covered sitting area.

PRECEDING PAGES Large casement windows and doors fully open this library to the outdoors. To protect the books from the elements, they are kept under glass inside a weathered-teak bookcase made in India. For the upholstery, Scheerer chose beachy grasscloth and durable Sunbrella fabrics. The traditional wing chair and antique Windsor chair strike a historical note that's wholly appropriate in this former loyalist colony. **LEFT** The central hall of the house contains the stair to the master suite. Scheerer restored the Cuban tiles original to the house and replaced stair spindles with a colorful, graphic Chinese Chippendale lattice. **BELOW** This sitting area is all about natural materials and the way Scheerer uses them. He found room for seagrass, wood that resembles driftwood, wicker, straw, and cork, and a pair of cheery blue-and-white garden seats for contrast. **OPPOSITE** The trestle-base dining table is Brazilian, and the rattan and seagrass chairs came from a catalogue. Gnarled hunks of driftwood, hurricanes, and glass bottles adorn the tabletop.

ABOVE Scheerer found the patterned Cuban tiles in the original pantry and had them reproduced for the kitchen, where he installed them floor to ceiling, like wallpaper. RIGHT The countertops are white Formica, harking back to the 1960s, and the refrigerator is faux vintage—Scheerer didn't want to spoil the ambience.

ABOVE Scheerer reframed a group of colorful Haitian paintings that came with the house and hung them in a girls' bedroom. The painted wicker and wood table was also found in the house. The lamp's durable grasscloth shade suits the tropical environment.
OPPOSITE Twin four-poster pineapple beds were made of pickled teak in India. Scheerer dressed them in fresh white candlewick bedspreads, airy canopies, and pillows in a Muriel Brandolini block print. The striped rug is by Dash & Albert, a favorite Scheerer source.

LEFT AND ABOVE In a large guest bedroom, an inventive surround gives the fireplace prominence. Scheerer designed the framework in a stylized Dutch Cape architectural motif and filled it with blue and white *pique assiette*, or broken crockery mosaic. Walls are painted a deep brown to provide relief from the unrelenting tropical sun. Blue and white accents give the room buoyancy. Blue-black Cuban tile is cool underfoot. All the fabrics are by John Robshaw. **OVERLEAF, LEFT AND RIGHT** The second-floor master bedroom was overly large and lacked a logical place to put a bed. Scheerer's solution was to divide the room with a freestanding pecky cypress wall and tuck a little office behind it. An oversized channel-quilted headboard is attached to the wall. Oeil-de-boeuf windows line up with the front door of the house and contribute to an overall nautical feeling.

OPPOSITE With its shiny, painted-cypress paneling, the long, narrow master bath has a boat-like vibe. The bathtub surround is travertine. Bahamian palm-leaf matting covers the floor. **ABOVE** The spectacular view from the veranda off the master bedroom can be enjoyed while relaxing on a double-wide teak chaise longue. The woven-fiberglass chair is sturdy and virtually weatherproof. An inexpensive Appalachian home craft, Scheerer sourced it on the Internet and thinks it's just great.

Island Chic

IN HIS OWN LIFE, TOM SCHEERER'S BIGGEST INDULgence is the glamorous apartment he keeps in one of Paris's thick-walled medieval buildings. Before this French adventure, he had always avoided decorating in the French style in America because it risks seeming artificial. But now that he lives in France a week or so out of every month, that country's style is much more natural and nuanced to him, and if a situation truly calls for it, he's happy to summon up French chic.

In the case of this house on Harbour Island, Bahamas, the clients live most of the year in London, but the husband comes from an illustrious French family known for its superb houses. His uncle, one of the world's most famous twentieth-century tastemakers and couturiers, once made a media splash for having put American wicker in a seventeenth-century château.

"I wanted to give this house a beachy but also a French spirit," Scheerer says. "When I thought of my client's uncle, it was like having an all-seeing and very discerning eye watching us from afar—and not in a bad way! We wanted to please him."

Scheerer renovated the house and added a new wing of his own design. He connected the old and new parts with a breezeway that also acts as a dramatically vaulted dining room. His understanding of French chic clearly includes serendipity and a touch of Gallic frugality: he made the base of the ten-foot-long dining table from two sheaves-of-wheat rattan pedestals he found in the house and fashioned its top from leftover construction lumber, stained gray to match the architectural trim. The lineup of bamboo director's chairs came from a catalogue. "You can sit there in a wet bathing suit," says Scheerer, who knows that in Harbor Island it's customary to show up for lunch wearing only that.

At the entry to the new wing, Scheerer used an accordion folding rack to make a cheerful hat wall—another nostalgic summer-house vignette that he reprises often.

"My family's always had a hat room—I guess it comes from being fair skinned," he says. Under a rustic Chinese altar table are baskets of towels and other beachy essentials, ready for the grabbing. A Swedish Almoge chair, the perfect exclamation point, was tossed into the mix at the last minute. "I bought it many years ago in Bloomingdale's, of all places," he says. "It was just the right moment to give it away. It's a place where nobody would sit, but it's good for putting your bag down on."

The house's breezy French island style is perhaps most pronounced in the living room. Though Scheerer used utterly informal furnishings such as catalogue sofas, rattan-bodied, Baldwin-style slipper chairs, and a Formica coffee table, he imposed a strong overall symmetry that feels like inner balance. "There's something relaxing about a certain kind of hyper-symmetry," he says. "It gives a sense of stasis. It's particularly appropriate in a place where you want to stay cool and calm." French casement windows open inward. In front of them, tall wooden pedestals hold aloft bottle lamps like sculptures. It's a grandly arranged room, though there's nothing remotely grand in it.

A girl's pink and chocolate brown bedroom was done in much the same spirit. It has catalogue headboards and its tall canopies, bed skirts, and curtains were all made from new Indian print bedspreads. Scheerer simply used the bedspreads the way others use French toile, and it makes for a chic retreat. The back story is that at least part of this frugal stylishness was dictated by island economics. With astronomical tariffs on imports, Scheerer likes to either make things on Harbour Island or buy inexpensive furnishings and materials abroad. "In order to get the pink bedspreads we needed, we had to buy twelve dozen in mixed colors," he remembers. "So I got the bale of Indian bedspreads and gave away the blacks, yellows, greens, and blues. But at eight dollars each they were still a bargain!"

OPPOSITE Acting as architect on this project, Scheerer designed a new wing and connected it to the existing part of the house with this breezeway, which also serves as the dining room and passage to the pool. He made the dining tabletop out of leftover pecky cypress from the library's walls and set it on a pair of painted-rattan bases he found in the house. Bamboo director's chairs provide easy, comfortable seating that stands up to wet bathing suits.

ABOVE An open window from the kitchen to the dining breezeway doubles as a convenient pass-through for entertaining. Scheerer's wall-hung modernist shelving serves as a bar. **OPPOSITE** Vintage bentwood chairs surround a Saarinen tulip table in the kitchen. A triumvirate of materials—travertine floors, Cuban-tile walls, and horizontal cypress paneling—characterizes Scheerer's signature Harbour Island look.

Scheerer wanted every room in the house to feel truly open to the outdoors and to that end he had old-fashioned in-swinging casement windows made in France. Two walk-in pantries made it possible for Scheerer to eschew upper cabinetry in the kitchen, for a more spacious, less kitchen-like feeling. He covered the walls in Cuban tiles with a lacy snowflake pattern.

OPPOSITE The stair hall of the new wing is furnished with a Chinese console table and a green-painted Swedish Almoge chair. **LEFT** At the top of the stairs, Scheerer placed the house's only arched window. It was meant to suggest the atmosphere of a traditional house in Provence. **ABOVE** The painting above the stairs is a happy accident of color. It's an interpretation of a Kees van Dongen portrait of an Arab boy, and was a gift from the owner's uncle, a talented Sunday painter.

PRECEDING PAGES The living room's doors and windows were reproportioned and French-style casements were installed. On the exterior, angled Bahamian shutters shield the room from direct sunlight. The floating Formica coffee table was made in situ by local carpenters. The pair of sofas came from Crate & Barrel, and Scheerer piled them with a collection of print and solid pillows in varied shades of blue. **ABOVE LEFT** The coffee table is arranged with books, seashells, and games. **TOP RIGHT** A large hand-blown bottle lamp looks sculptural on its pecky cypress pedestal. **ABOVE RIGHT** Cubbies hold stationary, stamps, and postcards at the ready. **OPPOSITE** The secretary was designed by Scheerer and made to order by the Raj Company in India. Scheerer flanked it with a bamboo standing lamp and a fanciful peacock chair.

ABOVE Daybeds in a corner of the study with pickled pecky cypress walls sometimes accommodate overflow guests. The rattan ottoman is a modernist classic by Franco Albini. **RIGHT** An X-base campaign desk made to order by the Raj Company sits under a window between rows of Scheerer's signature wall-hung boxes, which here serve as bookshelves.

Though its walls are white, this guest bedroom has a vivid color scheme. Scheerer chose a favorite print, Schumacher's Katsugi, in a gold and mushroom colorway, for bed pillows and the bed skirt. The brass lamps are vintage finds from the Dixie Highway in West Palm Beach. Nineteenth-century palm leaf botanical prints in yellow-lacquered bamboo frames round out the color scheme.

BELOW AND OPPOSITE In this guest bedroom, the bed hangings, bed skirts, and curtains are all made from the same pink and white Indian print bedspreads. The headboards are from West Elm. A particularly nice vintage bentwood chair with loopy arms was painted white for graphic effect against the dark walls. Vintage French *os de mouton* benches serve as luggage stands.

Lyford Cay Club

SCHEERER'S SPLASHIEST PROJECT TO DATE IS THE refurbishment of a private club so Old Guard and sequestered it's a wonder those in charge allowed a photographer inside. But the Lyford Cay Club, the social engine of a privileged enclave in the Bahamas, couldn't keep its chic new look to itself. When the April 2011 issue of *Town & Country* with Lyford on its pages hit newsstands, the design world swooned at Scheerer's array of festive rooms, restaurants, and bars turned out mostly in the same nearly edible color scheme: confectionary pink and green with a surprising chocolate brown, a combination as pretty as an old-fashioned birthday cake.

Scheerer had walked in on a club with a somewhat disaffected membership and faded, if not disintegrating, decorating schemes clung to by its more conservative members. The magnificently proportioned space that the club calls its living room looked like a staid Mayfair drawing room with formal furniture, wan green walls, and unremarkable chintzes. Scheerer saw it as his task to conjure a keener, more tropical sense of place, one that would feel contemporary while still evoking the club's glory days in the 1950s and '60s.

"Club rooms are a tightrope walk. They have to find a balance between feeling homey and being public spaces," Scheerer explains. "They have to be at least as good as the members' own living rooms. They also need to have something that distinguishes them from a hotel."

He settled on a grand, sunny version of a Regency Revival style. "Let's call it Bahamian Regency," Scheerer says. "I didn't invent it. It exists, but it's different from the Hollywood version, being gentler, less kitschy, less glitzy. It has the charm of Brighton Pavilion, that look of Chinese Chippendale."

In the lobby, he kept the original sand-colored terrazzo floors and the towering antique mirrors in two corners. But by papering walls in faux driftwood and reupholstering the old curving sofas in a vintage-style fig-leaf print, this entrance hall was instantly rendered beachier and lighter.

As for the vast and lofty living room—the club's chief parade ground—Scheerer transformed it into what might be one of the world's all-time fabulous rooms. He repainted a bit of the old furniture and slipcovered sofas and chairs in a lighthearted print on cotton ticking with the blurry suggestion of damask. Grandly scaled India-made pier tables crafted in pickled teak worked wonders. His introduction of wicker chairs and hand-stenciled sisal carpets may have been deemed too informal by some members. But nobody could resist his master stroke—a chorus line of seventeen-foot-tall ivory palm trees hand painted on brown grasscloth walls. Traced from an Indian palampore document fabric, the tree silhouettes shoot up from the chair rail and turn the room into a frolicsome tropical performance.

Who knows if members even notice the dozens of small clubby touches added by Scheerer? He's a longstanding, omnivorous student of clubs everywhere. Looking as if they've always been there are new pagoda-topped vitrines in the lobby where the notices are posted, special towel-return bins made of teak with caning panels, and little mahogany shelves holding ironed linen hand towels above the sinks in the men's dressing rooms.

Embossed ashtrays shaped like sea grape leaves are an anachronistic and nostalgic touch. "It's my coup de grace: the Lyford Cay Club steal-able ashtray," he says. "They may need to order a couple of hundred a year because they do go missing, which is the point!"

Scheerer's decorating at Lyford has recaptured bygone traditions, invented new ones, and shored up membership. "It's a living and breathing Slim Aarons world, assiduously loved and preserved," he says. "Happily, I was able to help reinforce its strengths."

OPPOSITE Scheerer's tour de force is the Lyford Cay Club. In its living room, seventeen-foot-tall palm trees hand painted on chocolate brown grasscloth walls set an effervescent tone. The large teak console is one of a pair that Scheerer designed to sit under fantastical Italian gilt-wood mirrors, a gift to the club from one of its members.

ABOVE In the lobby, Scheerer kept the original antique mirrors in two corners. He repainted existing coffee tables white and re-covered a curved sofa in Peter Dunham's Fig Leaf print. For beachy charm, he added trompe l'oeil wood paneling and round sisal rugs. OPPOSITE Scheerer also made use of an original antique mirror in the outdoor poolside restaurant, here overlaying it with his modernist version of a Chippendale lattice to give the illusion of terraces beyond.

The club has a number of bars and restaurants, and Scheerer created a different atmosphere for each of them. **TOP** Atmospheric lighting and a predominantly red palette combine to make this bar a cozy retreat in the evening. **ABOVE** The bar in The Little Club sports Lyford Trellis wallpaper in brown and pink, and a jaunty striped awning. **RIGHT** In the Yacht Club restaurant, a sailfish presides over a crisp room with black captain's chairs and a nautical black-and-blue-striped floor.

RIGHT Scheerer designed a loggia for the cocktail hour that's entirely open to the elements. Canvas drops with clear plastic windows are rolled down in inclement weather. He used a mix of traditional wicker with painted furniture. The pendant lantern is of his own design, and the center table, with its wave-patterned frieze, was made in India. **BELOW** The club's eponymous sea grape–leaf ashtray can be found in every room. Don't you want one?

LEFT Scheerer refurbished the club's many cottages and guest rooms, giving each one a traditional base but also a fresh spin in various tropical pastels. In this robin's-egg blue room, he painted the existing furniture white and added airy bed hangings and testers, as well as chintz curtains. Curvy wing chairs provide an extra layer of comfort. **ABOVE** Scheerer outfitted the club's pool bar with a festive tented roof and a sorbet color scheme. He repainted the existing strapwork furniture white, added a white sofa with pink cushions, and designed the backgammon table with a pineapple base.

The Lyford Cay Club's living room reveals Scheerer's mastery of a new genre. Taking a fresh look at an old way of life, he merged relaxed comfort, vintage pizzazz, and real glamour. The redecoration of this room set a new standard for tropical resort style and for club rooms everywhere.

Sources

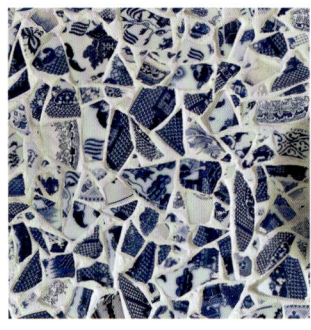   

Adelphi Paper Hangings, LLC
P.O. Box 135/102 Main Street
Sharon Springs, NY 13459
(581) 284-9066
www.adelphipaperhangings.com
HISTORIC WALLPAPERS

Akari Associates
32-37 Vernon Blvd
Long Island City, NY 11106
(718) 204-7088
NOGUCHI LIGHT FORMS

Amir Hasan
120 Carroll Street
Brooklyn, NY 11231
(718) 246-2926
SPECIALTY PAPERHANGING

Bamboo & Rattan
4900 South Dixie Highway
West Palm Beach, FL 33405
(561) 315-7295
www.vintagebamboorattan.com
VINTAGE AND CUSTOM RATTAN

Bauhaus 2 Your House
530 East 8th Street, Suite 102
Oakland, CA 94606
(888) 272-5331
www.bauhaus2yourhouse.com
MODERNIST REPRODUCTIONS

Beauvais Carpet
595 Madison Avenue
New York, NY 10022
(212) 688-2265
www.beauvaiscarpets.com
ANTIQUE RUGS AND
CUSTOM CARPETS

Bielecky Brothers Ltd
979 Third Avenue, Suite 911
New York, NY 10022
(212) 753-2355
www.bieleckybrothers.com
CUSTOM WICKER AND
RATTAN FURNITURE

Bonacina Vittorio
Strada Valassina 34
Lurago d'Erba (Como)
22040 Italy
+39 031 696119
www.bonacinavittorio.it
CONTEMPORARY RATTAN
AND WICKER FURNITURE

Brian Leaver
P.O. Box 1473
Amagansett, NY 11930
(631) 513-3967
www.brianleaver.com
DECORATIVE PAINTING
AND FINISHES

Bruce Erhard
4650 Georgia Avenue
West Palm Beach, FL 33405
(561) 588-7288
VINTAGE AND ANTIQUE
FURNITURE, DECORATIONS

Charles Burger
@ Quadrille
979 Third Avenue, Suite 1415
New York, NY 10022
(212) 753-2995
www.charles-burger.fr
TOILES DE JOUY

Christopher Farr
748 N. La Cienega Blvd
Los Angeles, CA 90069
(310) 967-0064
christopherfarr.com
CONTEMPORARY CARPETS

Corner House Antiques
599 Route 7, P.O. Box 411
Sheffield, MA 01257
(413) 229-6627
www.americanantiquewicker.com
VINTAGE WICKER FURNITURE

Cove Landing
22 East 80th Street
New York, NY 10075
(212) 288-7597
www.covelanding.1stdibs.com
ANTIQUES AND WORKS OF ART

DLGV Architects
224 Valencia Avenue
Coral Gables, FL 33134
(305) 444-6363
www.dlgvarchitects.com
ARCHITECTURE

Davis & Langdale
231 East 60th Street
New York, NY 10022
(212) 838-0333
www.davisandlangdale.com
20TH- AND 21ST-CENTURY
DRAWINGS AND PAINTINGS

Dryden Gallery
40 East 12th Street
New York, NY 10003
(212) 420-1690
www.drydengalleryframing.com
CUSTOM FRAMING

Frank Reijnen
1450 Second Avenue, 6A
New York, NY 10021
(212) 794-1610
DECORATIVE PAINTING
AND FINISHES

Gerald Bland
1262 Madison Avenue
New York, NY 10128
(212) 987-8505
www.geraldblandinc.com
ANTIQUES AND WORKS OF ART

Gill & Lagodich
108 Reade Street
New York, NY 10013
(212) 619-0631
www.gill-lagodich.com
ANTIQUE AND CUSTOM FRAMING

Hinson & Company
@ Donghia
979 Third Avenue, Suite 700
New York, NY 10022
(212) 935-3713
www.hinsonco.com
WALLCOVERINGS

Homeward Furniture
2912 V Street NE
Washington, D.C. 20018
(800) 616-3667
www.homewardfurniture.com
THONET REPRODUCTION
FURNITURE

JF Chen
941 Highland Avenue
Los Angeles, CA 90038
(323) 466-9700
www.jfchen.com
ANTIQUES AND MIDCENTURY
FURNITURE

John Derian
10 East 2nd Street
New York, NY 10003
(212) 677-8408
www.johnderian.com
DECORATIVE ACCESSORIES
AND UPHOLSTERY

John Robshaw
@ John Rosselli
979 Third Avenue, Suite 1800
New York, NY 10022
(212) 593-2060
www.johnrobshaw.com
FABRICS

John Rosselli
979 Third Avenue, Suite 1800
New York, NY 10022
(212) 593-2060
www.johnrosselli.com
FABRICS

Jonathan Burden
180 Duane Street
New York, NY 10013
(212) 941-8247
www.jonathanburden.com
ANTIQUES AND WORKS OF ART

Kevin Paulsen
311 Wall Street
Kingston, NY 12402
(845) 338-8046
www.kevinpaulsen.com
DECORATIVE PAINTING
AND MURALS

Lee Garvey Paper Shades
5 Dusenberry Road
Bronxville, NY 10708
(914) 274-8309
CUSTOM LAMPSHADES

Lee Jofa
979 Third Avenue, Suite 234
New York, NY 10022
(212) 688-0444
www.leejofa.com
FABRICS

Leonard's Antiques
600 Taunton Avenue
Seekonk, MA 02771
(508) 336-8585 or
(888) 336-8585
www.leonardsantiques.com
ANTIQUES AND ANTIQUE
REPRODUCTION BEDS

Loro Piana
748 Madison Avenue
New York, NY 10065
(212) 980-7961
www.loropiana.com
CUSTOM CASHMERE THROWS
AND FABRICS

Luther Quintana
114 West 26th Street
New York, NY 10001
(212) 462-2033
www.lqupholstery.com
CUSTOM UPHOLSTERY

Merrill, Pastor & Colgan
927 Azalea Lane, Suite B
Vero Beach, FL 32963
(772) 492-1983
www.merrillpastor.com
ARCHITECTURE

Morgik Metal Design
145 Hudson Street
New York, NY 10013
(212) 463-0304
www.morgik.com
CUSTOM METAL WORKS,
CURTAIN HARDWARE,
AND FURNITURE

Mr. Mom's, Inc.
www.wickerplantstands.com
(866) 933-0071
WOVEN-FIBERGLASS CHAIRS

Naga Antiques
145 East 61st Street
New York, NY 10065
(212) 593-2788
nagaantiques.com
ASIAN ANTIQUES, FURNITURE,
AND ACCESSORIES

Nazmiyal
31 East 32nd Street
New York, NY 10016
(212) 545-8029
www.nazmiyalantiquerugs.com
ANTIQUE RUGS AND CARPETS

Nobilis
979 Third Avenue, Suite 508
New York, NY 10022
(212) 980-1177
www.nobilis.fr
FABRICS AND WALLPAPER

O'Lampia
155 Bowery
New York, NY 10002
(212) 925-1660
www.olampia.com
CUSTOM LIGHTING

Peter Dunham/Hollywood
at Home
724 and 750 N. La Cienega Blvd
Los Angeles, CA 90069
(310) 273-6200
www.hollywoodathome.com
FABRICS

Phillip Jeffries
@ Holly Hunt
979 Third Avenue, Suite 503
New York, NY 10022
(212) 755-6555
www.phillipjeffries.com
GRASSCLOTH WALLCOVERINGS

Pierce Allen Architects
80 8th Avenue
New York, NY 10011
(212) 627-5440
www.pierceallen.com
ARCHITECTURE

Quadrille
979 Third Avenue, Suite 1415
New York, NY 10022
(212) 753-2995
www.quadrillefabrics.com
FABRICS AND WALLPAPER

R. E. Steele Antiques
74 Montauk Hwy
East Hampton, NY 11937
(631) 324-7812
www.resteele.1stdibs.com
MIDCENTURY FURNITURE
AND WORKS OF ART

The Raj Company
1-C, K. Khadye Marg
Mahalaxmi
Mumbai 400 034
India
+91 (22) 2354 2626
www.therajcompany.com
ANGLO-INDIAN ANTIQUES
AND CUSTOM REPRODUCTIONS

Raoul Textiles
@ John Rosselli
979 Third Avenue, Suite 1800
New York, NY 10022
(212) 593-2060
www.raoultextiles.com
PRINTED FABRICS

Robert Rich Associates
20 W. 20th St., Suite 900
New York, NY 10011
(212) 645-4631
www.robertrichassociates.com
ARCHITECTURE

Sage Street Antiques
114 Division Street
Sag Harbor, NY 11963
(631) 725-4036
ANTIQUES

Schumacher
979 Third Avenue, Suite 832
New York, NY 10022
(212) 415-3900
www.fschumacher.com
FABRICS AND WALLCOVERINGS

Scott Estepp Gallery
P.O. Box 19669
Cincinnati, OH 45219
(513) 237-6927
www.scottesteppgallery.
 1stdibs.com
ANTIQUES AND WORKS OF ART

Sears Peyton Gallery
210 11th Avenue, Suite 802
New York, NY 10001
(212) 966-7469
www.searspeyton.com
CONTEMPORARY ART

Sheila Potter Lamps
1416 Sam Rittenberg Blvd
Charleston, SC 29407
(843) 723-3649
ÉGLOMISÉ LAMPS, WORKS
OF ART, DECOUPAGE

Shyam Ahuja
201 East 56th Street
New York, NY 10022
(212) 644-5910
www.shyamahuja.com
FABRICS AND CUSTOM CARPETS

Sterling & Knight
979 Third Avenue, Suite 1010
New York, NY 10022
(212) 754-5880
www.sterlingandknight.com
PRINTED FABRICS

Studio Four
900 Broadway, Suite 201
New York, NY 10003
(212) 475-4414
studiofournyc.com
BROADLOOM CARPETS
AND TEXTILES

Tai Ping Carpets
860 Broadway
New York, NY 10003
(212) 979-2233
www.taipingcarpets.com
BROADLOOM AND CUSTOM
CARPETS

Tom Kirchhoff Architects
1907 Commerce Lane, Suite 106
Jupiter, FL 33458
(561) 575-9994
www.kirchhoffarchitects.com
ARCHITECTURE

The Urban Electric Co.
2130 N. Hobson Avenue
N. Charleston, SC 29405
(843) 723-8140
www.urbanelectricco.com
CUSTOM LIGHTING

Vaughan
979 Third Avenue, Suite 1511
New York, NY 10022
(212) 319-7070
www.vaughandesigns.com
LIGHTING AND FABRICS

Villa Lagoon Tile
15342 State Hwy 180
Gulf Shores, AL 36542
(251) 968-3375
www.villalagoontile.com
CUBAN TILE

Wyeth
315 Spring Street
New York, NY 10013
(212) 243-3661
www.wyethome.com
MIDCENTURY MODERN
FURNITURE

Yamakawa Rattan
Jl. Kemang Raya No. 24A
Jakarta 12730
Indonesia
+ 62 (0)21-719-3068
www.yamakawa-rattan.co.jp
RATTAN FURNITURE

Zuber
200 East 59th Street
New York, NY 10022
(212) 486-9226
www.zuber.fr
SCENIC WALLPAPER